Exploring Your
Inner Reality

Exploring Your Inner Reality

A Guidebook to Astral Projection and the Out-of-Body Experience

Jonas Ridgeway

Exploring Your Inner Reality

Copyright © 2013 Jonas Ridgeway

Portions of this book were originally published in digital format at JonasRidgeway.com.

All artwork is used by permission of the copyright holders: Cover art: PeopleImages. Interior art: timoph (TOC); Shannon Keegan, pg1; John Woodcock, pg9; Dominic Sata, pg11; Adrian Niederhäuser, pg23; Andrew Polushkin pg57; Mustafa Hacalaki pg85, pg165; Leon Bonaventura pg87; kimberrywood pg95; excape25 pg119; Jeffrey Thompson pg127; Elena Belyakova pg141; VLADGRIN pg147.

All quotes are used by permission (see credits, pg173).

Printed in U.S.A.

Published by Night Swimming Press
ISBN-13: 978-0615776965

Second Edition, January 2016

www.JonasRidgeway.com

for my mother

"Our ordinary consciousness shows us only one specific view of reality. When we learn to close off our senses momentarily and change the focus of awareness, other quite valid glimpses of an interior universe begin to show themselves."

– Seth

Table of Contents

Introduction

First, this book is being written for the beginner practitioner. I will assume your knowledge of the subject is limited and will thus offer a simple, step-by-step guide to leaving the body. Although "astral projection" is often used as a catch-all term for any conscious activity occurring outside the body, throughout this work I will make a clear distinction between etheric projections and astral projections (etheric projections being the most common, at least for me). By applying the same techniques I use, I believe that anyone can achieve the out-of-body state on a regular basis and with their full critical faculties intact. Surely if I can do it, you can do it (*if you really want it*). It is only a matter of conditioning, allowing yourself to see the "door" that you never noticed, to realize the freedom that you never knew you had – to edge pass the threshold and beyond matter.

To be asleep doesn't equate to being unconscious. Indeed, you are never actually unconscious while you sleep, only using a different portion of consciousness. There is no reason why you can't bring along your everyday waking self into the sleep state, save for ignorance and an untrained psyche. While your body slumbers, you can be as awake as you are right now reading this. There is no natural law preventing you from doing so. As a species we have largely disconnected from our inner lives to where most of us are unaware that this other reality – this nonphysical reality – exists. If we remember anything at all after sleeping – places, faces, remnants of conversations – we always assume it to be a byproduct of the brain, self-created, based in non-reality, a dream, and so disregard it. Consequently, we remember less and less of what actually takes place during the night, and not all of which are dreams.

You have the means to connect consciously – your regular waking awareness – to this other reality via your inner bodies and retain the experiences. This is your divine right, and it is expected of you. These finer, higher-vibratory bodies automatically separate from your physical body during sleep and are controlled, usually, by an inner you of which you are largely unfamiliar. As you sleep, this inner you is attuned to the astral realm, where you dream, and engage in various other activities that you likely don't recall upon waking or that your brain translates only as fragmented dreams. With a little coaxing, however, you may take full conscious control of your astral body – or body of light, which it is sometimes referred to as – and explore your inner reality. Alternatively, and perhaps best for beginners, you may use your etheric body for a more earthly experience. To whichever subtle body you shift your consciousness, your outlook on your own existence will be transformed. The bottom line will be clear: You are more than flesh and blood. There is no death. You will always exist, whether

you have a physical body or not. As my favorite author Seth says: "...
you are 'dead' now – and as dead as you will ever be."

I was fortunate enough to have been raised by a mother who was
open-minded. She wouldn't just automatically dismiss any idea or
belief that appeared too wacky to be real. She would give it her consideration, study it, arrive at her own conclusion, or leave it open as a
possibility – never allowing the masses to dictate or decide what was
real and what wasn't. Without her in my life, I don't know if I would
have been as willing to listen to those who say they can willfully leave
their bodies and travel the earth and cosmos. I might have labeled
them as kooks or delusional nut cases. Despite having several paranormal experiences as a child, without my mother I might have "grown
up" and spent my life scoffing at those who believed in anything that
wasn't an established fact by the scientific community. If man's ma-
chines and tools can't verify something, it doesn't exist, right? Thanks
to my mother, I know better.

I think for most of us as we leave childhood we tend to move
farther away from the inner aspects of ourselves. As adults we have
unwittingly sealed off this passageway and our belief at this point has
been solidified that life is PHYSICAL and there's nothing beyond that.
Those who tell us differently, are, unfortunately, and unintentionally,
muddying up the spiritual side of life with disinformation about an
angry god, damnation, and an eternity spent in hell.

Consequently, many of us have come to the following conclusion:
you live, you die, the end. Your thoughts are merely brain tissue or
brain-states and you will cease to exist once your time is up. The clock
is ticking. There's no logical reason to consider anything more. We are
essentially squishy bags of blood with no souls, marching towards
death and the big sleep from which we will never awaken. Man up,
face reality, prepare for nonexistence. This is what the atheists tell us,
to embrace science and renounce the outdated, old-fashioned belief of
a god overruling and judging us all. It's progress in one sense, but
slams and locks the door in another. Unfortunately, with no god to believe in, atheists can't fathom life beyond the physical (to consider that

would bring them uncomfortably close to those "church-goers", and besides, science says if it's not physical it can't exist). So, here we are, stuck with the heaven-and-hell folk who got God all wrong, and the atheist "realists" who can't be bothered with afterlife considerations.

Clearly, if you want to bust through all of this, you'll have to put down your stubborn doctrines and dogmas. In order for us to access our inner life consciously we must discard our restrictive convictions. We have essentially cut ourselves in two, a disconnect of our everyday conscious self from what we consider merely our dream life. There is a whole other reality of yours that is just as real (and more expansive) than your physical one, as the physical one could not have formed without the other. If you are dead set against the possibility of this other reality then you have sealed yourself off from it (that is, from your everyday ego's standpoint). You must be open to receive it. Being adamant or rigid that no life can exist beyond the material world will only ensure that your ego will remain thus oriented. The best research-er is one who will consider all angles, even the seemingly ridiculous and outlandish, as it may lead to something unexpected. Those who scoff and assume without examining are those who tread a narrow line with blinders on.

Since your physical senses are all that you are accustomed to using, it may seem highly improbable to you that there are other planes of reality interpenetrating the same space as the material plane -- but this is something you can verify personally with sincere intention and prac-tice. Even while attuned to physical reality your eyes don't see everything that is around you, such as radio waves and ultraviolet light. We should not be so quick to assert that something is impossible just because our scientists haven't discovered it (and aren't even look-ing for it), especially since man has made claims of traveling outside the body throughout recorded history.

Having a physical body can be likened to wearing an antique deep-sea diving suit, heavy and cumbersome and designed to function in a specific environment, only able to view what is immediately in front of you through the glass portal window of your helmet. When you project your consciousness away from physical reality you have essentially re-moved this bulky diving suit and have attuned to a new set of senses and environmental laws. Flight is now possible, 360 degree vision, en-hanced memory, timelessness, dual consciousness, instantaneous travel, etc. You have switched from a lower frequency body to a higher one, where matter – to a large extent – no longer matters. (I say to "a large extent" because there has been a few occasions while out of body where I had difficulty moving through objects, for whatever reason.)

Without a nudge in the right direction, it is easy to overlook or never realize the inherent powers we possess. I believe as children we were all more attuned to our inner senses (such as intuition and heightened perceptions) but as time passes these senses become less apparent. Look back at your childhood (when you were more recept-ive) and you may remember a few odd events that, at the time, you had been certain had actually happened – but now, as an adult, you have disregarded them as childhood "make believe" because they don't fit in nicely with your known reality. You grew up, donned that business suit, and have forgotten your native inner faculties. For me, after having had hundreds of fully conscious out-of-body experiences and other paranormal matters, I can look back when I was younger and make better sense of the bizarre memories I have.

My favorite odd memory that I recall I must have been around five or six years old. I remember being awake and crawling across the ceil-ing, stopping at the glass light fixture in the center, then crawling back towards a barrier that divided the room from the next. That was it. It had seemed so starkly real but it didn't make any sense so I called it a dream. Could this have been my first conscious projection? It would be many years later before I would do such a thing again!

I've had other experiences in that same old house that were rather trippy. In this example it was night and I was in bed. I saw a male figure in a suit enter my bedroom after having walked straight through the wall. I was awake. To be able to see this vision I must have been using my second sight / etheric sight. The figure walked towards me and then disappeared. Of course I screamed bloody hell for my parents to wake up and comfort me.

My mother also had an incident in that house. She would hear crying in the middle of the night and would get up and check each of our bedrooms but we would all be asleep. Only she could hear it (my father never heard anything). We found out later that the house had once been a nursing home (most likely many old people had died there). A woman my dad spoke with at the time said our home was known to be haunted and she would never consider going inside it. My dad never told any of us this until many years later. The house has since been torn down.

Although I hadn't heard the crying in the house that my mother had, I did often hear voices that only I could hear, and it happened usually when I was in deep concentration, such as doing my homework or drawing. I'd be scribbling away while a voice or several voices would whisper hyper-encouragements to me. I had assumed that this was normal. (An RCSI psychiatric study done in 2012, using a pool of 2,500 children aged between 11 and 16, reported that up to 1 in 5 children between the ages of 11 to 13 heard voices. As children got older, however, these voices would stop.)

Then there was my ability to pick up my mother's thoughts on occasion, which would give her a bit of a shock. I had a knack for intuitively knowing what she wanted, be it a particular object or book, or me just being the catalyst for an answer about something she was seeking.

Today I have a different perspective on these type of experiences. To see or hear strange beings in my home will always be unnerving or even frightening to some extent (depending on their behavior), but at least I understand it now. Just remember this – whenever you're alone, you may not be; there are other lives on alternate frequencies who may well be occupying the same space that you are currently, and if you happen to be in the right state of mind, you may catch a glimpse of them and what they are up to.

If learning about out-of-body travel and other metaphysical subjects is fresh new territory for you, you should be in for some truly life-changing events. By just reading material of a spiritual nature it can stimulate your inner senses and get you primed for a variety of awe-inspiring experiences (that is, if you have an open / receptive mind). My mother observes light shows whenever she gets deep into her studies. She can see this phenomenon whether her eyes are opened or closed. She calls them "her purple lights". The purple lights tend to swirl about, like clouds moving but in fast-motion. It always coincides with her metaphysical studies; the deeper she studies, the more intense the purple lights become. It may be due to her crown chakra being stimulated as the seventh chakra relates to spiritual awareness or higher consciousness.

Aside from the pure joy of being outside your body, there are other reasons you should learn astral projection or out-of-body travel. For one, shifting your consciousness away from physical reality will allow you to better understand how the material world exists *because* of inner reality, and how everything is interconnected. It is easy to think this is nonsense if you don't acknowledge that you are a spiritual being first. We are learning that we form our reality. The objective physical world is not the product of a god apart from you but the handiwork of an incredibly connected sea of entities (our whole selves) working on a supreme level that our conscious outer ego is not aware of or privy to. The consciousness that you know is but a mere shadow of your whole entity, which is but a part of the constantly unfolding energy that is everything. God is not this unchangeable (or completed) being distinct from the universe, that you are at the mercy of. God is you, and the others, and everyone else. But God is also the totality of every being, of all consciousness en masse (All That Is).

When you slip out of your skin and see the power at your proverbial fingertips, then you understand more clearly that our physical reality is the ever-changing expression from all of us via inner action. Forming this reality is engineered individually (by one's beliefs, desires, emotions) but also as a unified whole, moving and acting and creating together (expressing itself to know itself), an intimately-connected school of fish in a self-created cosmic sea. Whether in body or out of body, if we want to function effectively we must acknowledge the power of our thoughts.

So, let's get on with it – you want to know if out-of-body travel is real. Once again, you will require an open mind if you want to experience it (an open mind is an open doorway). Skepticism is good to a degree but you will have to allow at least a crack in the door of possibility or the experience will not present itself to you. Don't build a roadblock if you want important data to reach you. Once things begin to happen it will be a domino effect. Your old ideas about reality will be altered rather briskly – blown to bits, really. It takes only one fully conscious OBE (out-of-body experience) to dispel any notion that the physical world is all there is. It will become abundantly clear to you that the blueprint for consciousness survival is etched into each and every one of us, that life is never-ending, that our present time on earth is but a blip on an infinite scale of what is yet to come. After your first OBE you will be irrevocably changed. You will have joined the "afterlife bandwagon" and you'll be urging everyone else to come aboard – you now have this insatiable, incurable *impetus* to tell any stranger off the street about your OBE, everyone you meet, to any one who will listen. Yes, you've become rather annoying, but screw it – you can't help it.

Separating your consciousness from your body is more fun and exhilarating than probably anything you can do on earth, and there is the potential for a lot of self-growth by doing it and exploring this boundless inner reality. It will certainly change your physical life for the better. Indeed, the world would be a better place if everyone would take a conscious peek behind the veil at least once to witness their true infiniteness (or deathlessness), and to reawaken those memories of where we all originated. We are unlimited beings. Anything is possible.

PART ONE

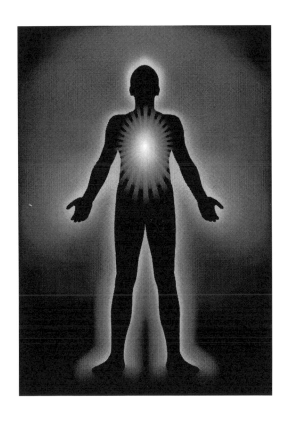

How It Started: My First Out-of-Body Experience

I was a teenager when my mother first told me about her out-of-body experiences. She would gain consciousness after having spontaneously separated from her body during sleep. There she would be, floating above her bed with no clue as to why or how this was happening. Initially these were not pleasant experiences, for they made her question her mental and physical health (she knew these weren't dreams and so believed that something was seriously wrong with her).

Later she learned that she could walk through walls, and fly. Because my own mother had experienced OBEs, I knew the phenomenon to be real and needn't rely on the testimonies of strangers in books (who could I trust more than my mother?). Since I could take this know-ledge for granted, I believe this to be a key factor as to why the OBE presented itself relatively easily to me. Later on, when she had given me more details about her OBEs, I was hooked; and it wasn't too long after that that I was sharing stories of my own.

But before my first fully conscious OBE I was for months com-pletely obsessed about it. I read everything on OBEs or astral projec-tion that I could get my hands on, starting with Robert Monroe's *Jour-neys Out of the Body* (this was the book my mother had first read on the subject; before reading it, she'd been so troubled by her experi-ences that she had actually seen a doctor about her condition). After reading Monroe I moved on to Muldoon, Fox, and carefully studied everything Jane Roberts' Seth had to say about it. By now my subcon-scious was so inundated with the idea of OBEs that it was only a matter of time, I thought, before I would awaken outside my body, or during the process of leaving it.

However, several strange happenings occurred before my first OBE. I began to experience what I soon learned to identify as remote viewing. I'd come awake, acutely conscious, with the ability to see an-other location with my mind's eye. In the beginning it seemed several hours of sleep was a prerequisite for such an occurrence, but later a vision could develop from a mere nap (although this was much more rare). At first the vision was almost exclusively of an unpaved road, either of dirt or gravel, which moved beneath me as if I were flying above it a few feet from the ground. I knew this wasn't an OBE; I knew I was in my body, on my bed, in my room. I was remote view-ing, which was like being somewhere without actually being there. It was mesmerizing. The road would continue, flanked by trees and brush; sometimes mountains were in the distance … the details were all there. And I found that I could "move" faster with a mere thought to do so, or slow down.

Once, seeing through my eyelids, I had a vision that at first did not involve any motion. The image was of a stand of trees. When I wondered what was to the left the vision instantly shifted to the left and continued on, like a camera panning the area: more trees, then a man came into view. He was middle-aged, wearing overalls, and had a long gray ponytail. Using my will, I kept the "camera" on him as he walked. Soon he was standing in front of a brown horse; a woman stood on the opposite side of the animal. Then the vision faded and I came out of this deepened state.

Sometimes I have visions of the past – of our old house, of my brother and sister as young kids. These are not still frames but moving pictures, complete in detail and in full color. These animated images would stay steady and clear as long as my concentration didn't fluctuate. The farthest into the "past" that I know of is when I remote viewed what must have been the apatosaurus dinosaur (two giants moving among the vegetation; the vision was brief but one of my favorite RV experiences). Also, sometimes I would glance into what appeared to be from a possible future. For example, I once remote viewed a full-color map of the world. I could move the map with a mere thought, to any part of the world I wished. I located the United States and found that it had changed, that some of the coastal states had shifted or broken apart from the mainland, transformed into separate islands (perhaps this broken landmass effect was actually due to sea-level rise caused from global warming).

Another time, just as I was awakening, I saw some strange writing in black in an unknown language on my ceiling. This is the first and only time it happened in quite this way. Normally when I see writing it is in book form, thrust in front of my sight as though by some being just out of view.

Sometimes I would see through the eyes of a stranger, seeing everything he or she was seeing. I once watched a woman drawing for several minutes, not as if I were looking over her shoulder but as if seeing directly from her eyes. Another time it was from a boy's perspective (I know intuitively things about the person immediately, such as their gender, age, emotional states, and other things.) In this instance the boy was running down the hallway to class, and when he got there he shuffled around a bit and then took his seat. Kids were chattering loudly (I can hear in many remote viewings but not all of them), and then the boy and I were watching a girl at the front of the class who was giving a speech. As she spoke, she scribbled away on the chalkboard. This vision was in full color and as real as if I were actually in a classroom.

Sometimes the experience can be a bit morose or make me feel sad for the individual (e.g., a young girl by herself in a wheelchair in an empty room). Another example was from the eyes of a police officer (I knew he was a police officer intuitively and I could see another officer next to me). We were at the front door of an apartment building. The main vision was of an old brown wooden apartment door, except to the left was an officer with a police dog at his feet. The dog was quickly let into the apartment as the door was flung open. We rushed in, and there was an overweight man in a white t-shirt and dark gray pants who was standing with his back to us. I was upset that the officer had let the dog loose on him when the man appeared to be not resisting. The dog bit the man's left ankle. I saw immediately a wooden table that the man had been standing next to. On the table was a single bullet and a revolver. I got the sense that the man had intended to commit suicide. All of this happened quickly, in a matter of moments, and as clear as if I were really there.

To have visions like these while fully conscious make me believe that these are real happenings that I'm tuning into. They are so highly detailed and seemingly independent of me that I'm convinced I'm seeing actual events. I am even considering that these individuals may be my reincarnational selves (simultaneous lives; offshoots of my whole self), as Seth teaches.

It is interesting to note that I'm not locked or stuck into anyone's perspective. I could veer off if I wish it. And I'm not controlling anyone's movements in any way. When I'm looking around it is me looking around, not me making someone look around. I'm not controlling anyone's eyeballs, for example. But I can easily look in any direction if I desire it. I can move the perspective to anywhere but it isn't necessary to move my physical eyes to shift the scene. I do it that way because it feels as though I'm physically awake (but I'm actually in trance) and it's natural to move my eyes to see a different perspective. I could just think "look left" and that will work fine but it's much more natural to just look around (however, it does strain my eyeballs because sometimes I look too far in a direction and it hurts a bit). When I am seeing through someone's eyes and that someone is in motion, my perspective changes along with them; I go where they go, I'm along for the ride, and I see what they see, unless I decide to look elsewhere.

I've had remote viewings directly from the eyes of a wide variety of people. For the most part there doesn't appear to be any rhyme or reason as to why I'm seeing through a particular person. The majority of my remote viewings actually are not from the perspective of anyone; it is me alone that is seeing. To experience one, sometimes I do nothing more than look at the empty space in front of me and then the moving images appear. At first it is only faintly outlined imagery, as is common with most people while resting, but then it can develop into a crystal clear vision (usually this occurs during a deep trance state after having first slept several hours). I have nearly given up on the notion that these visions are some sort of message to me personally (except for a few that were obviously meant for me). It is seemingly random, as though flipping through tv channels, but I won't rule out some sort of connection.

Not only is it possible to see directly through the eyes of another person and intuit many things about them, it is also possible to apply this inner sensing to other living things besides people. Seth calls this "Inner Vibrational Touch". Having done this spontaneously with people, I was inspired to try this with plant life and was successful with my first attempt. During a mind awake / body asleep session, I put out the suggestion that I wanted to know what it felt like to be grass. That was all it took. Swiftly, all at once, my perspective dropped to the ground and I became grass. Or, more accurately, I was sensing what it was to be grass. Surprisingly, I could see – it was quite bright, sunlight shone down on me, and grass surrounded me. I could actually feel an intensity as if I were feeding off the sunlight. And, most surprising, I could feel myself growing / extending (I don't know how this sensation of growth could occur in this short time frame, unless the timeline had been sped up so that my experience of being grass would be all-encompassing).

I have had many experiences of clairaudience where I hear random voices but without any visual data. This is similar to remote viewing (or clairvoyance) but you aren't tuning into the picture. During the mind awake / body asleep state I will begin to hear conversations between several people. Just random, usually boring conversations that you might hear on the street or in any restaurant. Or I would hear people I know, such as my parents having a long conversation even though they were many miles away in another city. When hearing these voices there is often a knowing of who these people are (even though they are often strangers to me), and what these people look like, but it is not done visually. It is difficult to explain but it's like a packet of knowledge of who they are is dropped into my head but without any visuals in the normal sense.

Although most of the voices do seem disconnected from me (unaware of me), there have been instances where I feel the people speaking are fully aware of my presence but are not addressing me and don't seem particularly interested in me; they are talking about random things near me, their voices encircling me as though they are adults huddled around a sleeping child, perhaps unaware that the child is awake and listening (such as the time when I'd heard a man and two women discussing at length the dire state of the world). And then there are the voices that are clearly addressing me or trying to relay information to me, or those strange whispering voices I heard often as a child when in deep concentration, who would bombard me with their overly enthusiastic encouragements. Or the time when I heard a woman (who was not visible) say to me in a sing-songy voice: "I *heeeeaaaar* youuuuuu!" – as though I were thinking too loudly and perhaps annoying her (she was probably just being playful).

Symbolic imagery will also likely make an appearance for you. Since my mind during this time was so highly focalized on the idea of OBEs, the symbolic visions that bubbled up were on topic and were obviously meant as an aid to me. One example, the "Sandman" vision, was a three-dimensional representation of Man (it appeared as a model, or a glass mannequin). He had a water-type valve and spout attached at his ankle from which sand or dirt was flowing at a quick rate. As the sand poured from the spout, I could see that the level of sand in the body itself was dropping (in the same way that an hourglass empties), until, shortly, there was nothing left but a clear shell of a human form. I took this demonstration to mean that the sand represented the matter of man's physical body, and when the matter was removed (leaving the body), what remained was one's subtle body; perhaps showing me that, with knowledge and practice, the projection of one's consciousness is really as easy and as simple as turning on a faucet (shifting one's awareness away from the physical form).

Another example of symbology making an appearance during my OB practice centered around an old-fashioned louvered glass window. I was lying on my back after having slept around eight hours, hands high on my chest, got the cricket sounds, fully conscious, could see through my eyelids. The cricket sounds continued to get louder. An open book was suddenly placed in my field of vision but I couldn't read it as it seemed to be in another language. I tried to make sense of it for quite some time. Then, abruptly, the book was pulled away (perhaps this unseen presence was trying to teach me something important but I was too dumb to read his book).

Next, a three-dimensional image of a glass-louvered window appeared. Just the window itself, hanging in space, nothing else. I continued to stare at it – it was as real and as detailed as though I were looking at it physically. I didn't know why it was here, or if there was some meaning attached to it. Then there was movement – the second pane or slat of glass started to shimmy a bit, to loosen itself from the rest of it.

It was sliding down and then it separated completely from the whole window and fell away. At the exact moment that this happened, as the second slat of glass separated entirely from the rest of it and was falling, I became "unhinged" from my body. *Oh Yeah!* I was quite happy and excited because it had been so synchronized and effortless – I had left my body without consciously trying to do so. As far as the window itself, I surmise that I was being shown that each slat of glass represented a higher vibrational state. I didn't count how many slats of glass there were but I'd say at least six or seven, maybe more. Was I being taught to visualize this louvered window each time that I wanted to go out of body, to select a vibrational state or different state of consciousness by choosing the corresponding slat of glass? I'm not entirely sure what this experience was about but it was certainly interesting. Although I'd left my body during this session, this was not my first OBE (we'll get to that next).

With the preceding paragraphs I have given you an idea of what you may experience before your first OBE. During your projection practice, you can definitely count on a wide assortment of auditory and visual stimuli that may shock you out of your trance-state if you aren't expecting it. Just be prepared for it, and when it happens don't overreact, observe it calmly and see what develops. Although I didn't experience it prior to my first OBE, the vibrational state is also common during one's early OB practice (I will discuss this in depth in the forthcoming chapter "Out-of-Body Predicaments").

My first fully conscious OBE was preluded by one of these seeing-through-the-eyelids episodes. I came out of a deep sleep after eight hours and was seeing through my eyelids, through the far wall, and into the kitchen. It was as if I were peering through a small hole about three or four inches in diameter, darkness all around but a crystal clear image within (as I learned later, my mother would also sometimes remote view in this same manner – darkness surrounding a small hole with a clear image within). Now, peering through this hole, I was looking at the kitchen faucet. It was as clear as if I were standing there. I could see the way it sparkled where the sunlight hit it. I could see my mother, her back to me at the stove. She was cooking something. I saw a pan and what looked like a cake in it, and a white box of something on the counter. Afterwards, I found out that she had been in the kitchen cooking at the same time that I had had the vision, and that there was a white box on the counter in the same place with nothing near it as I had seen it (it was a box of donuts). And finally, although it was meatloaf she'd made for my father, the resemblance was that of a cake.

Because of Oliver Fox's book *Astral Projection*, I owe it to him for my first conscious out-of-body experience. In it, he had described the very thing I had experienced several times, of seeing through one's eyelids. But what struck me was the part where he said OBEs could be achieved quite easily from this state if one thought to do so. After seeing the vision of my mother in the kitchen, I did think to leave my body. I thought simply that I would like to roll off the bed to the right and onto the floor – and no sooner I had done just that, leaving my physical body behind! It was amazing; it worked so fast and effortlessly. Like a book opening, my second body simply flipped over and down onto the carpet.

My first reaction was how quiet it was outside the body, how even the act of projecting had been absolutely devoid of any noise (this would not always be the case, as my forthcoming projections proved quite noisy at times). My next reaction was how calm I was. I had no fear. My body was on the bed and I on the floor, but I wasn't afraid of dying. I knew what was happening.

I was on my hands and knees, staring at the carpet. I reached up with my right hand and touched the bed. I was thinking, *Cool. Cool. I'm doing it. Cool.* I was trying to remain calm, I didn't want to mess things up. My vision was foggy, but I could see well enough to move around the bed (I didn't think to look at my body). Walking, it felt as it normally does for the most part; I could even feel the "muscles" in my ankles and the bottom of my feet! This was quite surprising as I had never heard or read of anyone feeling this in their nonphysical form. I knew the second body would often mirror the physical in appearance but it hadn't occurred to me that common physical sensations could be replicated as well. I presently believe that there is an etheric equivalent or counterpart to every part of the physical body, inside and out. Or, perhaps it is the other way around – the etheric body being the blueprint for the physical body.

Now, as I stood at the foot of the bed I thought of my mother and how she'd said *"... you can go through walls"*. I decided to try it, but just as I was starting through the north wall everything went black, frightening me, and a second later I was back in my body.

Although I was upset that I had cut my first OBE short, it was a valuable lesson. As you will quickly learn during your first projection, the power of thought is the foremost principle to recognize. In the out-of-body state everything is ruled by it. Your thoughts will be acted out instantaneously (if you aren't careful), and thus maintaining mental control can seem an impossibility. You may bounce willy-nilly all over the place if your thoughts spin out of control. The trick is to keep your mind blank until you are ready to give a command. For example, in the beginning of the above experience, stray thoughts were absent because my mind was preoccupied with the word "cool", which I was repeating. At the end of the experience, as I was going through the wall, the fear of the sudden darkness put my survival instincts at play, catapulting me back to my physical. Thus, if you want to stay outside your body for as long as possible you cannot be a mouse afraid of a cat around every corner. You must come prepared, and be as even-keeled as you can manage. If I had kept calm the experience would not have been terminated.

So, again, the key to maintaining the out-of-body experience is to have control of one's mental activity (thoughts, emotions). Until you fully realize that out-of-body travel is safe, that you can't hurt yourself and nobody can hurt you, that your only impediment to a long and joyous trip is your belief in dangerous circumstances (where none ever exists), you will not be able to stay outside your corporeal shell for any extended periods. As a physical creature it is not easy to turn off our fears. We are so used to thinking in terms of "physical" that we bring all of those fears along with us, and often manifest unfortunate situations. Being brave in the out-of-body environment is a learning process – baby steps, testing the water. The more trips you have outside your body, the more at ease you will be for your next one. It will never be ho-hum, big deal, I'm a ghost again, but you do get more used to it and learn to suppress or to reduce the frequency of those emotional surges. It's all about getting comfortable in this beautiful boundless playground, with all of the new freedoms that you have. At the beginning you will be like a little kid on the first day of school – it can be overwhelming, but then you adapt (sort of).

Questions & Answers

1. How long will it take for me to have my first out-of-body experience? How long did it take you?

It took me a while (a few months). I'd spent a lot of time on the wrong path (for me), trying to leave my body before having slept first. I had read about yogis who would sit in a lotus position and meditate, and were able to leave their bodies that way. I would lie down and go through these relaxation techniques that were rather boring and meticulous, or listen to expensive audio programs that were supposed to ease you down into the correct condition for projection. None of this worked for me. I later realized that the easiest and most effective way to get my body conditioned for an OBE was to sleep for six to eight hours beforehand.

How long it will take you to have your first OBE is impossible to gauge. Everyone, of course, is psychologically different and thus exiting the body consciously will be easier for some and more difficult for others. Getting your physical body properly conditioned is only the first step; how you handle your thoughts and emotions while in this state will determine if you will be able to project. The slightest twinge of fear or hesitation will keep you from passing over that magical threshold.

2. When the term "astral projection" is used, does that mean that the astral body is projected to the astral plane?

No. The astral body is already on the astral plane, just as the physical body is on the physical plane. You do not actually "project" to planes but rather focus or tune in to specific planes. You become aware, or gain a different perspective (away from physical reality). Your other bodies are all right there with you, interpenetrating one another as each are of a different frequency. To become aware of another plane or region and to use its corresponding body, your consciousness needs to vibrate at that higher frequency. You will then be shutting down your physical senses and tuning into your inner senses.

Technically, there is no "leaving" the body to "travel" to another "place", as all "places" exists as one and so "distance" doesn't actually exist. Nevertheless, when you are focused away from physical reality you will experience distance often (and perhaps primarily) but going from "place" to "place" can be instantaneous by shifting your attention to where you want to be (you do this by focusing on the energy or essence of the person or place you wish to visit). Doing this effectively and consistently, however, is easier said than done. In my experience, the more conscious you are, the harder it is to get to a location instantaneously, often leaving me no choice but to engage in long-distance traveling. This is probably only my issue (my thought patterns / mental hangups interfering with me) and may not affect you.

3. Are there always sensations (such as vibrations) before leaving the body? What about sounds?

Not everyone experiences vibrations. Some report no sensations or sounds prior to an OBE; they simply slip out of the body. This is often my case (and it was for my first OBE), but I have had many experiences where extremely strong vibrations occurred prior to leaving the body – vibrations that were so quick and violent that it would only be a matter of moments before I would be flung out of body. These vibrations never hurt. In fact, I would sometimes have a mental laughing fit during these atom-shakedowns because the experience is so bizarre and ridiculously dramatic.

When I am experiencing these extreme vibrations I hear a loud roaring or rushing sound that hits its crescendo just as I am propelled out of body (which can sound like an explosion or a bird squawking). However, at the beginning of the vibrations I will sometimes hear what sounds like crickets. (I will cover this topic more fully in the chapter "Out-of-Body Predicaments".)

4. Will drugs help me to have an OBE?

You may be able to lift the veil, so to speak, and get a glimpse of the Other Side, but you do not want such an artificial inducement. You need a clear mind and drugs and psychotropic plants will cause confusion, disorientation, and will falsify your perceptions. None of my OBEs were induced by drugs. If you have a real desire to experience out-of-body travel then that desire (and practice) will get you there.

5. After I have my first OBE, will I be able to have them from then on?

Usually if you experience it once you will experience it again, if you still have the desire to do so. However, if it was an unpleasant or frightening experience you may never (consciously) project again. If you lose interest in OBEs that, too, may dwindle the number of conscious projections or even stop them all together. Desire and practice are the keys to projecting regularly and recalling them.

As before stated, the human species was not meant to be so divided from our physical life and spiritual life. Our full consciousness is meant to be able to flit in and out of different realities. Being able to leave your body consciously is not some forced voodoo that you shouldn't be doing. You are not going against the grain. You are simply getting back to where you should be, getting reacquainted consciously with all aspects of your being. Unless, however, you are the sort of individual who sees a lot more negatives in life than positives, or wallows in sadness frequently. In this case, you are presently unfit for conscious projections – such a mindset would only ensure harrowing or troubling experiences. This would especially apply to those with a mental disorder or emotional instability as a conscious projection could lead to additional stress / unrest.

6. Does out-of-body experiences prove life after death?

Yes and no. For those who have had an OBE with total consciousness, it is proof enough – the answer is usually an emphatic *YES!* Finding yourself apart from your physical body and still fully functioning (with your self-identity completely intact), still able to see, hear, touch, even smell and taste, still able to do everything and more, it is hard to believe that life wouldn't go on after death. In most of these people's minds there is little doubt, and in my own as well.

However, technically, no, it doesn't prove it. When I project, I still have a living body – perhaps when my physical body dies my consciousness will die with it, but I know that's not the case. I feel intuitively that we will survive, and I've come across other beings that I feel strongly were not hallucinations manufactured by my psyche. I've also seen many of my dead pets while OBEing (which I'll describe in detail later in this chapter). The fact is, there is no scientist on earth who can explain what consciousness is. There is no compelling theories for how the physical body can create it. Anyone who says that consciousness cannot survive death is making a wild assumption based on nothing.

Those who have had a fully conscious OBE come away with the conviction that what they experienced could not have been a dream, and you can't shake them from this stance. What is fascinating is how during my best OBEs my consciousness is more bright and awake than my everyday in-body consciousness. You really do feel as though you are alive for the first time. It's as though our physical bodies, being comparatively crude instruments, can only manage to utilize a smaller portion of consciousness (as if all of the lights haven't been turned on). That's not to say that just because you are out of body you are suddenly more intelligent (although I do have access to what appears to be the stored databank of my subconscious mind, which I'll discuss later in the chapter "The Astral Jukebox"). I'm just as slow to learn new things while out of body as when I'm physically oriented. You are the same flawed person as before, and uniquely you in every way, but one's higher aliveness does seem to be in attendance. I feel cleaner, less bogged down. Simply more awake.

7. How will I know that I had an out-of-body experience and not dreaming?

If you weren't fully conscious then you may doubt it and slap a "dream" label on it (although you were probably out of body while dreaming, as this is natural). When I left my body for the first time I was full-on AWAKE. Imagine the level of consciousness you are using right now, then imagine – at the *least* – that same consciousness outside your body. That's how the best OBEs are. As I indicated earlier, you will feel even more awake and alive than when you're physically awake.

If I were to tell you right now that you are asleep and lucid dreaming, you would laugh and say "hogwash!" because you know with every ounce of your being that you aren't dreaming – YOU KNOW THIS – and no one would be able to convince you otherwise. It is the same with a fully conscious OBE – you are certain that you aren't dreaming. The level of consciousness one uses with a lucid dream is not of the same quality as that of an OBE. In addition, the consciousness you use in a lucid dream is hovering more or less above or around or is pushed back from the scene of that which you have created, unlike an OBE where your consciousness is firmly situated at the exact location where you are at (much in the same way that you experience consciousness when you are physically awake). It is likewise with remote viewing – I am aware that I am in bed, in my room, and my consciousness is situated around my physical head.

So, to be clear, when lucid dreaming, consciousness is not as bright as an OBE and is somewhat displaced or has permeated throughout the content of the dream (not localized); it is as though you are a puppet-master from afar. These are two of the major differences between OBEs and lucid dreams. (I will discuss this subject further in the chapter "Objective Reality or Lucid Dreaming?")

8. What is the difference between astral projection and an out-of-body experience?

Astral projection is when you have tuned in to the astral plane. An out-of-body experience is considered by many to be only those experiences where you have left your body but are still close to the physical realm, which would be categorized as an etheric plane projection (such as when you are in your bedroom, flying over your town, etc.); that's not to say you can't see a semblance of the physical realm while in the astral plane, you can – but the astral is more prone to forming wild psychological meanderings. In other words, you won't, for example, see a two-headed monkey riding a unicorn while you are attuned to the etheric plane. Personally, I think the term "out-of-body experience" should be all inclusive for any experience where one's consciousness has moved away from the physical body to another "higher" vibratory body and environment.

9. What is the difference between an out-of-body experience and remote viewing?

In an out-of-body experience you are apart from the physical body, receiving visual and other data as you move about to specific "areas". With remote viewing you are still in alignment with the body, receiving images usually in front of or slightly above the eyes. Remote viewing is like being someplace without being there. When you are remote viewing, there is no question that you are still in your body (you sense your surroundings, such as your bedroom; you know that you are lying down and what position your body is in, etc.), and you know that you aren't dreaming. Your self-identity is intact as well. Everything is fairly normally except that you are aware that you are in a deep state and are seeing with your mind's eye.

For many, remote viewing is easier than leaving the body because the separation anxiety issue is not present, and, in my experience, remote viewings occur more spontaneously and more often than conscious out-of-body experiences do (but a remote viewing is often a precursor to an OBE when one has the inclination towards separating).

10. Is it possible to get lost during an OBE?

You may get lost, or confused about where you are (this will occur often), but it is not something to be concerned about. You will have no problem getting back to your body at any time. When you want to go back – you're there! It takes minimal thought power (the slightest desire) and you will be home again. Even if you aren't ready to go back your subconscious mind ultimately has control. If it senses any issue with your body it will call you back. If there is a loud noise or commotion in your physical vicinity, you will zip back instantly and awaken.

Your subconscious is extremely vigilant and responds to your emotions – if you put out signals that you are frightened, distressed, uncomfortable, etc., it will reel you in. This is not to say you can't have any emotions while out of body (a crying fit of joy will not send me back). But if you start to sound the alarm bells, signifying that something is wrong or that you are fearful, and if you express within that emotion the slightest twinge of homesickness, then your subconscious will take action. Thus, expressing fear alone is not the trigger; it's when it's coupled with the merest hint that you want to go back, or you have the thought *I can't handle this*. The subconscious mind will not let you (the conscious ego) experience more than you can manage, like a mother allowing you to walk to town for the first time – it will allow it, but if you become distressed or panic-strickened, it will sweep you up in its arms and take you back home.

11. I've heard that some projectors have had trouble waking up their body after coming back after an OBE. How common is this?

It's true that at times waking up physically can be tricky. The first time it is quite alarming, but don't panic; it's no big deal. If you should find yourself back in your body but unable to move it (often referred to as catalepsy or sleep paralysis), the best thing to do is just relax and try to let your consciousness dim. If you leave things alone your subtle body will align itself with the physical automatically as your awareness begins to fade.

Before I had known this secret I had had a couple of terrible experiences (terrible only because I had overreacted). The first time that I had found my physical body in this paralyzed or incapacitated state I panicked big time, screaming like a baby, ejecting myself from my physical body several times and then jumping back into it, until, finally, I was able to physically move again. I was afraid to go back to sleep!

An alternative method of breaking catalepsy is to concentrate intently on your physical body and attempt to wiggle your fingers or toes. This should send a strong message to your brain that you desire your body to wake up.

12. How difficult is it to find a particular person or place while out of body?

It is easier to locate a person (if there are emotional ties) but if there is a place that you feel strongly about that could be just as easy. However, "easy" is probably not the right word. For me, at least, as I stated earlier, it is not necessarily a quick and simple process to locate a loved one or go to a particular place. Yes, it can be instantaneous (if you're in the right mindset), but often what happens is this: I put out my intention (that I want to visit someone, or go to a particular place) but my etheric body is not quite ready – it pauses for a few moments like an outdated computer (*processing, processing),* and then suddenly decides on a direction and I begin to fly. I don't know why this happens sometimes and not other times, other than I must have some underlying thought channel that is hampering my conscious intention. I want to be there *instantly!* When it insists on doing it the slow way, I usually say screw it and stop the process because I don't want to have to fly all of the way there. I think my etheric body is a bit daft, or needs a tune up.

13. What if another entity takes over my body while I'm gone?

You are the only being who has the "key" to your body and only you can activate it unless you willfully give permission to someone else (such as what Jane Roberts did with Seth). Even if you give this permission or allow it, you have not lost control of your body, you are still connected to it, but now you are on the backburner, so to speak, while another being communicates through you. Some random spirit is not going to jump into your body while you're out and run amok with it – you leave your body during sleep every night (whether you remember it or not) and your body is still in your possession, isn't it?

14. If I go out of body when I sleep and I don't recall the experience, where did I go?

Beats me. There are any number of things you could be doing while OBEing. At times you may project from your body and wander aimlessly about in the astral plane, acting out your dreams; or just hover slightly out of alignment of your physical body while you sleep, recharging (so to speak). Other times you might meet with friends, family, and loved ones whose bodies are asleep as well, or meet with someone who has died (perhaps someone from another life), or attune to your various personality offshoots that are living their individual lives apart from your own (simultaneous lives), or do a myriad of other things that are specific and important to you as a person. You may be attending Soul School (as my sister calls it), learning from those more advanced or developed than you (spirit guides / masters), or communicating with your whole self to find the solutions to your earthly concerns.

You may have noticed that the problems in your physical life, large or small, can often be resolved once you "sleep on it" – this is because you had acquired the necessary knowledge or solution during the night by accessing your so-called higher-self or greater you (these solutions are usually passed down to you in the form of dreams). This is one example why it is important to have a dream journal and to use affirmations for dream recall.

As you can see, you are quite active in your "sleep" life – a lot more is going on than just your physical body getting rest!

15. I know that telepathic communication can be done while out of body, but is normal speaking possible?

The first time I experimented in using my "vocal cords" while out of body I couldn't utter a sound. At other times I was able to speak but my voice was extremely gravely or guttural. And yet other times (most times), I could speak normally or sing better than I ever could in physical life. I don't know the reasons for these variations. I suspect, however, it has to do with my particular thought patterns at the time. If my hoarse voice was thought-induced it must have been subconscious for I was certainly surprised by it. I've also tried to make noise by stomping my foot to the "ground" and was surprised to hear a loud reverberating banging. Again, was this a thought-induced sound or a natural law of this plane? I believe it was the former, of course, just another thought-creation done subconsciously. But how strange indeed to hear such a loud banging echo across that otherwise whisper-quiet expanse.

When I talk to someone while out of body, or sing, I usually do it the same way that I do it physically – open my mouth and let the words come out. It's primitive, surely, and a bit silly (it's like trying to fill your lungs with air to breathe when air is not needed and doesn't exist here). I'm used to being physical, to open my eyelids to see, to move my legs to maneuver, etc., and to mouth the words to speak. For me it is natural, because my ordinary waking consciousness is not yet used to this environment. I suppose after death one adjusts more fully to nonphysical reality, wherein telepathy and instantaneous travel become the norm.

16. My OBEs are too short – how can I stay out longer?

The hardest part to having an out-of-body experience is not getting out of body but *staying* out of body. A real annoyance while projecting is the sensitivity that comes with full consciousness. Of course, absolute total wakefulness is what you'll want while outside your body but that very alertness is what makes it difficult to stay out – you tend to overreact to situations, the slightest fearful reflex can propel you back to physical reality without a moment's notice. To extend your out-of-body adventures you need to acquire confidence and face your fears.

I have never heard of any projector doing this, but my best technique for staying out longer is by singing. You can also play subconsciously-stored music to accompany your singing by simply willing it (something I have a real knack for). Singing just keeps me level-headed as I move about or fly around. I think what it does is keep my mind preoccupied so that I don't get too exuberant over every little thing and thereby extending my trips. I also talk to myself – just mumbling like a crazy person. It seems to help.

As I am the king of overreacting, going through objects has often been one of the hair triggers that will send me reeling back to my body due to my thoughts about it, such as will I get stuck inside a particular object (I have done so a few times), or apprehension over what or who is behind a wall or door (objects do not appear transparent). I over-think things and make situations troublesome when they needn't be.

I may be the only projector who finds the following as a solution, but I found that purposely flying backwards helps greatly if you have difficulty going through objects (if your conscious mind can't wrap itself around the concept of going through objects, then you may not be able to). I do this to prolong my trips, and for the silly experience of it. By flying backwards, somewhat leisurely (and without using 360 degree vision), I'm not able to see which objects I'm going to pass through until I've passed through them. There is no fear, then, because I don't have a clue as to what objects were in my path until after the fact.

Flying backwards is actually calming, to just watch as the objects pass through me. If I'm a bit higher I may pass through tree tops, lower and I may pass through homes and various buildings (I've seen a woman sitting cross-legged on her bed; a man sitting on his couch talking on his cell phone; factory workers bustling about). What you do is lift slowly off the ground vertically (standing up) and just think of yourself moving backwards. A gentle glide is best as it doesn't heighten your emotions or alarm you. Yes, flying backwards is ridiculous, but if you have trouble passing through objects because of a mental barrier and need help in prolonging an OBE, give it a try.

17. Do animals survive death? Do they have souls?

We had a horse named Tonka that had died from old age. He was a shy and gentle creature. A week after his death I was traveling out of body over our field when I spotted him below. He had spent most of his life in that field and it is the same field where he was buried (to this day you can see a bright green patch of grass where his body fertilized the ground).

When my dog Jiffy died, I went out of body and found her in her favorite spot (near the back of the couch). She was sitting upright looking at me and I gave her a big hug. She was as solid as if she were still physical (I could feel her bristly fur as I hugged her). I was so happy to see her.

My cat, Mona, once followed me around during an OBE (she was physically sleeping on my bed with me at the time). It's kind of funny how we were both out of body at the same time, walking around together on my parents' property. She seemed content in this environment as though she were used to having conscious projections (perhaps this is the norm for animals, to slip in and out of realities while maintaining awareness throughout).

When my sweet cat Kiki-Marie died (she was 16 years old), the following morning after she was buried I found her sitting on my chest! I was in the mind awake / body asleep state and there she was, facing me, just inches from my face and as real as in physical life.

More recently I saw another one of my departed cats (Froggy), that had died of old age. Usually when I see my dead pets they look healthier and somewhat younger than when they had died (which is usually the case with people) but this pet was a little different. In physical life he was a huge fluffy cat but in the afterlife he took the form of a kitten.

We only had him when he was fully grown so I'd never seen him as a kitten, but here he was, sitting on the porch (always his favorite place), an incredibly cute little fur ball looking up at me. I gave him a pat on the head and said his name and he sat there staring at me. In physical life, although he was a big cat, he was as gentle as they come (he was afraid of mice), and I guess he identified or thought of himself as a kitten in the afterlife.

Robert Monroe has also reported something similar. In the out-of-body state he had once seen and recognized three of his pet cats that had died within the previous three years; they were hanging around right outside the house.

You don't necessarily have to be out of body to see your departed pets. You may be in the mind awake / body asleep state (still within your physical body) and be aware of them close by (or sitting on your chest, as the case was with Kiki-Marie). Sometimes they will jump on your bed suddenly and startle you, as happened recently with one of my dead cats when she hopped on the bed and then sat on the window sill above me (her favorite sitting place while I'm in bed). Or you may just get a vision of them being somewhere in your room (even though you may be prone on your back with your eyesight pointed upwards, you can still receive full-color visual data of where in your room your pet may be and what they are currently doing). Or you may hear them without seeing them. One of my cats hardly ever meowed in life but she had a distinctive chirp noise that she'd always make – without exception – when jumping onto my bed or lap. In the afterlife she still does this sweet chirp sound that I can hear while in an altered state as she jumps onto my bed, her way of greeting me and letting me know she's here.

As anyone with pets knows, they are all individuals with their own unique personalities just like us. I have no doubt that our animal friends survive death. I know the gulf between the living and "dead" may seem wide but you will see your loved ones again, including your pets. They are all much closer than you may realize. Even if you aren't able to consciously project, you are still likely in contact with them while you sleep, which is another good reason to write down everything you remember as soon as you awaken.

"The animals share with us the privilege of having a soul." – Pythagoras (c. 570 BC - c. 495 BC), Greek mystic, philosopher, mathematician, and "Father of Vegetarianism".

18. Does being vegetarian help with leaving the body?

There are some who say adopting a vegetarian or vegan diet will aid in leaving the body, and others who say it doesn't matter. The only thing I can say definitively was that all of my OBEs and remote viewings occurred on a meatless diet (I was a vegetarian for years and then became a vegan).

In the Journal of the American Society of Psychical Research, Prescott F. Hall wrote: "A vegetable diet tends to loosen the vibric matter of the astral body ..." I do often notice the vibration of my subtle body not only while in an altered state but also during normal waking consciousness, and it can be quite pronounced. Is this common for everyone, or perhaps a trait of a meatless diet? Do I have an unusually "loose" subtle body? I can be sitting or walking or lying down relaxing and I can usually feel this pleasant wavering that can be increased on up to a swaying sensation with minimal mental effort (although I still need hours of sleep before I can project). In addition, listening to some particular music with headphones on will also rev up this sensation. I've always thought of it as "The Whomp-Whomp Thing", which I will discuss in depth in the forthcoming "Techniques" chapter.

I think a meatless diet is something to consider given the association of vegetarianism and spirituality throughout history. We all leave our bodies effortlessly during sleep whether vegetarian or not, but the ability to do so consciously may be another matter. Perhaps vegetarianism does raise one's vibrations to where it allows for an easier conscious separation, although I doubt that all of these writers with books and courses on astral travel are all vegetarians (or vegans) – maybe a few. However, as some yogis have stated, if one does manage to project but has a physical body that is coarse (not refined by a plant-based diet), his consciousness may be regulated to the lower planes.

Although not specifically referring to vegetarianism, Seth taught that being in excellent health was a vital ingredient for promoting conscious projections. He acknowledged that OBEs can occur in less healthy individuals but stressed that an abundance of energy was necessary for acquiring stability.

So, bottom line is, I don't know if there is an actual connection between a vegetarian or vegan diet and conscious OBEs but I think it is worth considering.

19. Is the astral body the soul?

No. The astral body is no more the soul than is the physical body. Both of these forms (the physical and astral) are vehicles for consciousness, to function effectively on their respective planes. Nor is consciousness the soul. I believe we are multidimensional beings with more than one consciousness, more than one personality (our soul is the impetus behind each of our individualized offshoots, other selves of which we are unaware for the most part). Imagine a string of multicolored Christmas lights. Each uniquely colored bulb would represent a form of consciousness expressing itself differently, but all bulbs (all consciousnesses) are connected or linked to the electrical cord (which, as a unit, along with the bulbs, would represent your soul or whole self). Your soul is responsible for giving you consciousness, much like the electrical cord is responsible for giving light to the bulbs. You can follow this analogy further by thinking of electricity itself as the energy or force (God / All That Is / The Source) behind everything. As stated in the Introduction, the use of the word "God" here is not meant in a biblical sense.

20. How many bodies do each of us have?

It is believed that we are equipped with at least the following bodies: the physical body (with the etheric double residing on the highest subplane of the physical); the astral body; and the mental and casual bodies (the causal body residing on the upper mental plane). All of these bodies take up the same space, yet vibrate at a different rate. The higher the rate of vibration, the finer or less substantial the body – the physical body being the most dense, the casual the least; and each designed specifically for (and from) that specific plane.

Most likely, the etheric double is the body you will be primarily attuned to as a beginner practitioner to leaving the body (that is, if you are consciously inducing the separation process; if, however, you have learned to awaken during a dream state, which is more difficult, then you will find yourself within the astral plane).

Some of the older books state that the etheric double is not a vehicle of consciousness but rather a sort of maintenance station for the physical body. However, according to Seth, when you are projected, the physical body is still being maintained by the body consciousness, which consists of the separate consciousnesses of every atom, molecule and cell (which make up the consciousness of each organ).

21. What is the difference between the etheric plane and the astral plane?

The etheric plane is the highest subplane of the physical world and consists of finer matter or rarefied energies that cannot be seen with physical eyesight. There are four grades to the physical plane (solid, liquid, gaseous, and etheric), and the etheric subplane can then be divided into additional grades (super-etheric, subatomic, and atomic). When I go out of body and do some earth roaming I'm on the etheric plane (a.k.a., the upper physical plane), or, as Robert Monroe referred to it, "Locale I" or the "Here-Now". After projecting, the physical body is said to weigh less (about two ounces, according to some, and less than an ounce, according to others) as the finer matter of the etheric body has been displaced from the physical body. Seth also states that the weight of the physical body decreases when projection occurs, although minutely.

The astral plane is next on the vibratory chart (as before stated, all planes interpenetrate one another but occupy the same space). The lower astral plane is that area of the astral world which is closest (vibratorily-speaking) to the etheric plane, and where, supposedly, lower-vibratory creatures or negative entities dwell. Since I have not had too many negative entity experiences (hardly any, really) I think most of my astral experiences must be on the mid or upper astral plane (or perhaps the mental plane), which were those experiences that didn't involve what can be found in the material world, or were bizarre (such as meeting my younger self, which I've done twice), that bend time perception, or those large expanses where no "objects" could be found. Usually in these type of experiences I would suddenly AWAKEN to find myself there (no conscious decision to get there), unlike my etheric plane projections where I'm fully aware of the separation process (I just roll out of body and off the bed – there is normally no consciousness blackout or blink-off point during the whole experience, of separating, exploring, and returning).

Whatever the circumstances, if I'm out of body and conscious then I am overjoyed (to say the least), and ready to have some fun. Although technically incorrect, I often refer to my OBEs as "astral" trips for convenience's sake (and because the term is more commonly known), even though the majority of my travels have been on the etheric plane.

22. Can those beings residing in the astral plane go "lower" to the etheric plane?

Yes. Although they are no longer physically oriented and no longer have an etheric body, they aren't restricted to staying in the astral. They can create a pseudoimage of themselves and be seen etherically by others. This is how the so-called ghost or phantom is able to appear on the etheric plane despite their etheric body having long since "decayed". Many of these individuals are so distraught with their physical body's passing (or are unwilling to leave their loved ones behind) that they are determined to remain as close to the physical plane as possible, which is what is seen occasionally by the living and referred to as hauntings. Pets, as well, will often stay close to their human companions long after their own deaths.

23. What is it like to see your physical body during an OBE?

It's a freak-show and you're the star of it! The first time I looked at my sleeping face during an OBE I was shocked because I appeared dead (slack-jawed; face muscles relaxed; the eyes closed, which was the creepiest characteristic as this is not something you would normally see unless in a photograph). It's hard to describe the feeling of seeing yourself from this vantage point, face to face as it were. You see your body as it really is, for what it is, a machine, a vehicle designed for earthly exploration and experience. Conversely, you also get a deep sense of something akin to parental feelings. It's like looking at some young child or animal sleeping that you want to protect. It seems so vulnerable, lying there sedately without its consciousness. However, as noted earlier, it does retain a body consciousness that keeps it functioning properly while you are away.

If you can see your physical body during a projection (or, to be more accurate, the physical body as it appears from an etheric vantage point, which should not be confused with the etheric body which you are currently using as a vehicle for your consciousness), you are having an etheric plane projection (which is the top-most area of the physical plane). When you are attuned to the astral plane you won't be able to see the physical body at all.

24. How far can you go out of body?

In essence, there is no limit to how far away one can go from the physical body. However, there are "higher" areas that you do not readily have access to unless you are spiritually developed / able to vibrate at that frequency. You cannot visit a higher vibratory plane in a lower vibratory body, of course.

In addition, the condition of your mind plays a crucial role as to how far away from your body you will get. For example, extending my reach beyond earth on the etheric plane has proved difficult. I've been wanting to explore other planets and galaxies, but my particular mind-set is blocking me from doing so (I can only get so far skyward before panicking). There is no reason why I can't do this other than my psyche is preventing me. Contrarily, space exploration while semi-conscious isn't a problem – you can doing anything while semi-conscious or half-awake, or in dream mode. The problem occurs when I'm 100% wide awake and not dreaming. The experience is simply too real and my psyche flips its wig every time. I have enough problems just skimming across the landscapes while fully awake so space travel is a big step for which I am apparently not ready. (More on this later in the chapter entitled "Out-of-Body Predicaments").

25. Are things solid to the touch while out of body?

I've touched many things during my OBEs. The sensation of touch can be perceived in the same way as it is physically, such as feeling the rough texture of tall grass on my hand as I walked through a field (on my parent's property) in one of my earlier OBEs. I've also picked up small pieces of paper, leaves, etc. (I'm referring to the counterparts to these objects or its etheric equivalent; I have not been able to move anything on the physical plane, although I have tried). I've grabbed tree branches (usually during desperate crash-landings!), crawled around on my bed, walked up steps, turned doorknobs and opened doors, etc. But the question is, did all of these objects appear solid to me solely because of my beliefs? I've certainly felt the solidity of walls on my fingertips, but I've also felt walls give in, too – an odd sensation of resistance as I try to pass through it – and yet at other times it was as if there were nothing there at all.

My etheric body seems to be more dense on different occasions. This could be due to my thought-patterns, or, perhaps, my vibrational frequency is too low. Sometimes my etheric body feels so dense that passing through walls seems impossible (I would panic and back out as soon as I felt I was getting stuck). If it becomes too dense and sluggish I will go back to my physical body, less substantial and I can pass through objects with no resistance (such as when I'm flying). To be on the safe side I always throw my hands up before walking through a wall in case I have trouble going through it.

It is difficult to discern whether it is a vibrational rate issue (my etheric body just being too dense to pass through objects easily), or if it is caused by my subconscious or conscious expectation (for example, on some level I may be thinking that it is not natural to walk through walls). When flying backwards into buildings, I have never crashed into one – I am unaware of these buildings until I'm actually passing through them. This may lend credence to the theory that the solidity of an object is based on my belief, or it may be that in order to fly one has to raise one's vibrational rate to get off the ground and thus objects are at that point of a subtler nature.

When my intention is to pick up something I expect to be able to do so, and so I am able to (in actuality, that physical object never moved). Same thing with walking – I expect there to be a solid surface under my feet and so there is. Even in my first OBE, after I'd rolled out, I was able to touch the bed as I stood up (I fully expected it to be solid and so it was). But, interestingly, this doesn't always hold true, such as when I walked into the kitchen in another OBE and, out of habit, tried to turn on the light switch only for my hand to pass through it (I was *expecting* to be able to flick the switch but was unable to even touch it).

I think the sensation of resistance when trying to pass through an object may have to do with how slowly you go through it. If one is moving quickly, such as shooting through the ceiling, then it isn't an issue. On the other hand, if one is merely walking through a wall you may be met with some resistance.

As far as the etheric body itself, it is solid to the touch. I've touched and pulled on my tongue, stuck my fingers in my ears, licked my arm to see what it tasted like (yes, it was salty, extremely so that it startled me; I'm not sure if I detected the salt in my physical body via an inner sense or if this was a prank from my subconscious). You can also touch others who are in the out-of-body state (or those who have died and are no longer physically focused) and they will feel solid to the touch, just as though they were physical.

26. How do I avoid negative areas and entities?

If you put out negative vibes, you will manifest and / or attract negative entities. On the other hand, if you hold a loving or uplifting disposition, you will likely attract loving entities. The same principle of "like attracts like" applies for the physical plane as well. If you have a predominantly negative belief structure, you are going to experience a life that is predominantly negative or unfulfilling. If you do encounter something unfriendly while projected (of your own manifestation or otherwise), tell it to go away. If it doesn't respond accordingly, you can always go back to your body (your fear will probably send you back to your body anyway). If you continue to have this problem, the cure for you is to enjoy physical life more and the positive changes will be reflected while out of body.

It is important to remember that how you live your life, how you treat others, the thoughts you carry with you, the sum total of who you are, will determine the natural rate of your vibrational frequency. Thus, stop dwelling on every negative aspect in your life, stop being angry at those who may have treated you badly – get rid of your "hurt bag" that you hold so dearly to your bosom as though it were something of value. Toss it aside and stop playing the victim. Although anyone can have a conscious out-of-body experience with practice, you will not have a pleasant trip if you are prone to depression, anger, hate, and dark thoughts. Just as in physical life, you will attract circumstances that are consistent with your moral makeup and beliefs, and draw to you those of your own ilk or class (who oscillate at the same frequency as yourself). Find calm in your physical life and it will follow you while out of body.

27. What does the etheric and astral planes look like?

The etheric plane looks like the physical plane, for the most part. The main characteristical difference, in my opinion, is that it is much more vivid than the dense Earth. In the best OBEs it's as if everything sparkles (as though there are tiny pinpricks of light coming through everywhere). However, this may be due partially to the fact that in physical life I'm near-sighted (and refuse to wear glasses or contact lenses) so when I'm OBEing, and I have moved sufficiently away from my physical body, I have this utterly perfect vision that I'm not used to. I am simply stunned by how sharp and crystal clear everything is – the environment seems more real to me. To buzz over and in between a stand of trees at night with a sky filled with stars and a majestic moon is almost a sensory overload. You can't help but be in awe of the beauty everywhere. Furthermore, since my out-of-body consciousness is more acute than my physically-oriented consciousness, this may also account for the brilliance I perceive while in the etheric realm. Or perhaps I am just able to perceive a larger range of colors than my physical body is able to perceive.

Others have reported that the etheric plane appears hazy, dull / faded, having diffused light or lower lightness values, or they see only in black and white. These accounts are probably due to the OBEer being in a semi-conscious state, having not yet reached the optimal cognitive level and so the environment appears drab or as though one were peering through a screen or gauze. Once complete awareness has been attained the environment will open up fully.

With regard to the astral plane, the etheric plane transitions seamlessly into it so at first it may go unnoticed that you have further altered your consciousness or raised your vibrational frequency (the finer matter that makes up your etheric body will have coalesced or ρυ..ω .tself back into alignment with the physical form while you remain awake within the astral form). You will realize that a transition has occurred as the astral body's movement feels differently and the environment becomes more "creative" – don't confuse this with dropping into a dream state (although you may have). The astral world is extremely malleable and you can see the handiwork of your own complex thoughts as well as those of others.

28. Is there night and day while out of body?

When I roll out of body in the morning in an etheric plane projection, my room may be brightly lit. The sun rises as it does in any other morning. A nighttime projection is especially beautiful with an eerie, bluish atmosphere – like heavy moonlight – where everything tends to sparkle as I indicated earlier. Although it is night – and I may be deep in the woods somewhere – I am able to perceive the surroundings with a sort of hyper-realistic vision, as though wearing spectacles of an extraordinary strength. However, the somewhat spooky ambiance of a nighttime projection may not be ideal for the beginner practitioner (as you know by now, if you get frightened you will abruptly end your trip), so leaving the body during the morning may be preferable for at least your first few projections. That being said, if you project directly into the astral, or are in a half-awake state, it may be morning physically but appear as though it is night (and vice versa), or you could be in another part of the world where it is actually night.

29. What does the etheric and astral bodies look like?

The etheric body and astral body both assume a luminous, phosphorescent, bluish-grey elegance (my observation), and is usually close to an exact replica of the physical body, younger looking, for most, for this is how one tends to perceive oneself (this resemblance is constructed by subconscious thought, or your belief of what you look like). Similarly, if you harbor any negative body issues this may be reflected in your etheric and astral bodies (for example, if you think of yourself as being more overweight or less attractive than you actually are).

To the touch my subtle bodies are solid, and the entire body is highly detailed down to fingernails and the tiny hairs on the back of my hands and forearms (this really amazed me when I'd first noticed this!). As I mentioned earlier, you can even feel the "muscles" in your body (at least I can), such as when you walk. My "bits and pieces" are there, too (I have a penis! Yay!), as well as everything else.

There are a few discrepancies from others who have studied their etheric and astral bodies up close. Many accounts state that they couldn't see their subtle body at all. They existed solely as a point of consciousness and there was no outward appearance. Some see their astral body as oval shaped (which is perhaps its natural form). Others report having a wispy or gossamer-like presence, or a shape unlike the human form.

Perhaps my physical's "whole body consciousness" is largely responsible for me having such an accurate depiction of the human form in my subtle bodies. However, if this were the cause you would expect others to have the same observation (or, if good health is a primary factor then perhaps my clean diet may be accountable). On the other hand, since inward reality is expressed outward, the subtle bodies could be thought of as an energetic blueprint for the physical body, but if so, then why doesn't everyone see their nonphysical forms as completely as I do? It may well be that those who are more advanced (or have an indifference toward earthly life) have no need to visualize the human form while projected. In any case, I seem to have a knack for details. My subtle bodies are quite strong-willed and it would take a deliberate conscious effort to deviate from said shape.

Robert Bruce, in his online article "Treatise on Astral Projection", says that if you look at your hands, for example, they will melt away quickly (as a rule, he seemed to be saying). However, I have never experienced any melting of any of my body parts – on close inspection it remains solid, and no mental effort is exerted whatsoever in order to keep it this way. If anything, I would think looking at your hands would reinforce its form, not dissipate it, as you are drawing your attention to what you expect to be there – your hands. Thus, it seems the subtle bodies are quite individualized in how they behave (or the behavior is the result of one's expectations). If others have experienced this melting effect, it may be because they have read Robert Bruce's account beforehand. The mind is easily susceptible to suggestion (what you've read can become an affirmation to your subconscious). Although I have not experienced any "melting", the subtle body has an elasticity to it and can stretch quite far when willed to do so.

30. Are the etheric and astral bodies always "clothed"?

What you wear to bed that night is often what will be reflected onto your subtle body (via the subconscious mind) but not always – your out-of-body attire could be a three-piece suit with a top-hat, cane, and monocle. What you will be wearing depends largely on how you feel about clothes in general. If you are a woman in love with Victorian or vintage clothing, you may well find yourself clothed in such a way while projected. For me, since I have little interest in clothes in physical life (I usually wear board shorts and a t-shirt and I'm good to go), I am nearly always naked while projected because clothes make almost no impression upon me. This is also due to the fact that I don't wear any clothes while I sleep and haven't since I was a kid (I have trouble sleeping if I do). If I'm not naked while projected, I have noticed I tend to wear jeans with no shirt and barefooted. If you are concerned about roaming around buck-naked in the out-of-body state, don't be – this concern alone should be enough to prevent any unintended nudist romps. If you are naked and it bothers you, just think that you are clothed and you shall be.

31. Why do you prefer the rolling-off-the-bed method of projection over, say, floating out of body?

I use the rolling-off-the-bed method predominantly now because of habit. For the beginning practitioner, I think it is best to leave the body in a way that isn't too outlandish – floating out of body to me was just too strange a concept at the time. If I had tried it then, most likely any attempts would've been terminated the moment I'd felt a floating sensation. I'm a baby, what can I say? After you get somewhat used to the sensations associated with the out-of-body environment, having adjusted to all of the various speeds and modes of locomotion (flying, floating, gliding, spinning, etc.), and are comfortable with OBEs in general, floating out of the body will not be an issue for you. Initially, however, while you are learning and training, it is best to take the least abnormal avenue. You are building up confidence which is a crucial commodity for sustaining your OB trips.

32. Does the silver cord exist? Have you seen it?

I have always thought that the idea of a silver cord connecting the physical and the subtle body was a silly one, and I still do, even though I have seen it and touched it. This idea never rang true for me as being natural but instead an idea constructed by man to protect himself, to make him feel better and assured that while out of body he is securely tethered to the material world.

After reading about this cord in so many OBE books I wanted to know if it really existed. So, during an OBE I looked and ... lo and behold, I found it! It was thick and white (not silver) and connected to the back of my head. However, I still don't buy it. I've had enough experience with thought-creation to know how things can magically appear when one is "programmed" with certain ideas, although I will admit that it is interesting that my cord appeared white rather than silver or gray, this being contrary to all my reading.

Most likely this belief in a cord became popular because of the sensation of being pulled or yanked backwards when it's time to return to your body after a journey. It really does seem as though you are attached to a cord and being reeled back in. But in all of my OBEs I have never accidentally come across the cord; the only time was when I was actively looking for it, which makes me highly suspicious. One thing I've learned about the out-of-body environment is you don't want to search for things, you want to discover things. In other words, when you are looking for something specific you will almost certainly find it (that is, create it); those things in which you just happened to stumble upon are less likely to be one of your own thought creations, but not always. The psyche is so deep with so many hidden pockets that spontaneous creation can occur with no discernible effort. The good thing about an etheric plane projection is that the environment is relatively stable save for some inconsistencies and unintended thought creations now and again. With an astral plane projection, however, or while lucid dreaming, all hell can break loose at any moment, more or less.

33. Does it matter what position my body is in while trying to project?

I definitely think there's something about lying on one's back that helps trigger a conscious projection (although you can leave from any position). Almost all of my OBEs have been while on my back, and this seems to be true for the majority of projectors (see the results of my "OBE Survey" at the end of this book). I'm a side sleeper (fetal position); I can't sleep well on my back, so it's actually the slight uncomfortableness of lying on my back that allows me to leave my body. It's just uncomfortable enough that it keeps me from drifting too deep. It allows me to hover there in the right state and then I just roll out. (I automatically get into the back position in the morning, as though a part of me knows what it's doing.)

Try sleeping for six to eight hours, roll onto your back, and just let your consciousness edge down a few notches until you feel as though you are underwater yet maintaining your awareness. That's the point where I exit my body.

34. Have you ever done anything while out of body that you regret? Spying on people, etc.?

I don't spy on people, or try to pry into anyone's private lives. Yes, I have gone into many people's homes or apartments and looked around (I call it visiting, not spying!). Many times it was done accidentally, as I stumbled into some place (usually by flying backwards) or had suddenly appeared somewhere without any conscious direction (such as when I popped in at some cabin in which a grandfather and granddaughter were present). Other times I'll deliberately go into someone's house, such as my neighbor's, just for something to do (his was an old house, crowded with furniture, messy, a white ladder leading to a loft, which I climbed, and was hit with the smell of mildew; yes, the sense of smell is still available while out of body). Other than that, I don't snoop around too deeply in people's business. Unless you are a psychopath and unable to feel guilt, you wouldn't be able to get away with much, anyway. If you are doing something not in accordance with your own moral compass, then you will shoot right back to your body.

The only thing I've done that I now deem inappropriate and I regret doing was during my earlier projections I would go on these head-shaking rampages. The people that I came across while out of body had a tendency to ignore me, so my solution to this was simple: whenever I saw someone I'd grab their head with both hands and shake it back and forth, rather vigorously. Highly improper behavior; certainly not a friendly gesture. I just wanted to know if, by grabbing their head and shaking it, would this get a reaction from them. Turns out it does, for the most part. They looked surprised, confused, some amused (some smiled at me), and some were truly frightened. Some stared at me dumbly and didn't react. Many of these people were likely roaming around out of body or in a dream state and perhaps thought I was a demon or just insane (me being naked most of the time probably didn't help matters). Others might have been discarnates, or empty etheric shells left by those who had died recently.

I did this head-shaking thing many times, too many; it was kind of a hobby for a while. It was done out of an insatiable curiosity to know whether these people were real or merely expressions from my psyche. The amusing thing is, when they did react in some fashion or show that they were at least semi-conscious, this would often freak me out and thus send me reeling back to my body. The good news is (for everyone's sake), I no longer do this – my head-shaking rampage habit has long ended.

35. How is it possible that you can smell and taste in an OBE?

I'm not the only one who has experienced this. Oliver Fox as well has reported having a sense of smell while projected, and I have read other accounts. Since everything vibrates, a smell on the physical plane, for example, can be detected while projected via your corresponding inner sense. In other words, the vibration for that particular smell is identified through an inner sense and relayed to your consciousness as a "smell". Supposedly the first five chakras correlate with the five senses: smell (root), taste (sacral), sight (solar plexus), touch (heart), and sound (throat).

36. Is the sense of time different in the out-of-body state?

When you are focused away from your physical body beyond the etheric plane, one's sense of time is altered – you could be out exploring the nonphysical realms for what seems like a lengthy amount of time, only to return to your body, look at the clock, and see that little time has elapsed. In essence, it is like having your physical body cryogenically frozen, as the time you seem to be spending outside your flesh is not tallied against it (in other words, your physical body does not age at the normal rate during your astral trips). Similarly, you may experience dreams which seem to last many days or even weeks but in physical terms only a few hours had transpired.

In the truest sense there is no actual time or space. However, the closer you are to the physical realm during an OBE the more closely your regular perception of time is. If you are attuned to the astral or mental states, then time will be virtually "no time" or "free time" (an eternal NOW). If you are etherically focused, then time may seem similar to the physical realm or close to it. But, one's sense of time is highly subjective, and if you're only able to remember portions of an OB trip, then your sense of the duration of the experience would be off.

It is also possible to witness an event while out of body that hasn't yet occurred on the physical plane (a brief glimpse of the future). For example, while out of body, in your room, you may see your cat jump from the bed, run across the floor, hop on a chair and begin playing with a belt you had laid there. Then, after having seen this, you transition back to physical reality and see this exact scenario play out again, almost immediately or within minutes. What you had seen was a probable event before it had actualized physically.

There was man who attended a Gateway session (at the Monroe Institute in Virginia) who reported that during a remote viewing he had seen a specific red car in front of the building, only to be disappointed to find out the car wasn't actually there after the RV ended. However, later that same day a red car appeared at the building that matched perfectly to what he had seen.

This phenomenon can also occur with sounds. For example, during an OBE (while I was asleep in a travel trailer), I heard this loud double-thump noise that shocked me back to physical wakefulness. About a minute later, the exact sound was heard again as my furnace door suddenly popped open and bounced twice on the hard linoleum floor (the furnace's wooden door opens from the top down). There was no question it was the same sound: a double-thump, wooden-y sound as it bounced against the bare floor. I got up and replicated the sound (dropping the door down and letting it hit the floor) and it bounced twice with the same loud tone as I had heard while out of body.

Sylvan Muldoon (the author of *The Projection of the Astral Body*), also describes this phenomenon. While out of body he had gone into the next room and was able to trip a metronome into motion. When he returned to his body and was physically awake, the metronome was off, but then within seconds it started up, seemingly of its own accord. (It is interesting that he was able to trip the metronome while projected; this is quite a feat as I have never been able to move anything physically.)

37. Is it wrong to leave the body just for fun?

Not at all. It is no more wrong than it is for you to have fun in your physical body. Some occult books (especially the older books) will tell you that your subconscious mind will not allow you to consciously project if the reason for doing so is frivolous. According to them, a lofty goal must first be in mind before one is set free (such as to meet a guide or to help the recently departed) but this is not true. *Play* is the building blocks of the universe, of everything. You may leave your body with full consciousness for the most mundane / silly / frivolous reasons as long as you aren't doing anything that would violate the rights of another, otherwise your subconscious – your moral integrity – would apply the brakes. If you simply want to go out of body for the fun of it, to do weightless acrobatics or to practice your air guitar skills atop the Great Pyramid of Giza, so be it, these are reasons enough and access shall be granted (as long, of course, as you understand and apply the basic steps for leaving the body). You are free to have an OBE to satisfy nearly any objective – from the most mundane or ridiculous to the most angelic of aspirations. It is the unscrupulous and dishonorable (not the frivolous) goals that will keep you from consciously separating from your body.

38. What happens after I die?

I believe it will go something like this:

After death, you will be temporarily on the etheric plane (a.k.a., the ghost world). This will be a transition area for you as you work through the trauma of having passed. You'll likely go through a denial stage, attempt to reanimate your body, try to contact your family, have a good emotional meltdown, then accept that your physical life is over. Some of you may be so traumatized by your death that you simply shut down, like a computer in stand-by mode. Your consciousness is on, but barely. It is not extinguishing itself, of course – you are just overwhelmed at the sight of your lifeless body and perhaps from the belief that you'll never be with your family again, or that you'll cease to exist at any given moment. It is all too much for you and your consciousness dials itself down, as a sort of protection mechanism for the health of your psyche. Then there are some of you who may be caught in a whirlwind of astral hallucinations, based on your beliefs and thought processes (e.g., your expectations of a specific afterlife – angels, heaven, hell, etc.– distorting reality). Others will be there for you, however – perhaps loved ones from previous lives, a friendly guide, or an OBEer passing by – to help you adjust to your new (and true) reality.

Your personality remains the same after death, and all of your memories intact. Even though this personality is only one aspect of your whole self, you will never lose this part of you – this one-of-a-kind identity – just because you have shed your skin. This particular personality will further gain knowledge and advance, as do all portions of your whole self.

You will still be able to communicate with the living in some fashion. Your loved ones will visit you in their sleep while out-of-body but upon waking they will scarcely remember it, perhaps only as a fragmented dream. They will, however, usually feel something pleasant had occurred during the night in connection with you.

Soon – in a matter of days – your etheric body will die as well (it is no longer needed since your physical body has perished) and then you'll make yet another transition, to the astral plane. Here you'll be surrounded by loved ones who have come to greet you. All of these individuals you recognize instantly, all of the memories of the lives you once shared together rush back to you. The love is immense, and it is as though no time has passed.

But, what's next? You may remain in the astral for a while – to take a breather, so to speak – then back to school / training on the physical plane. You'll have access to the knowledge gained from your previous lives, and after some serious self-reflection and with the help of guides, you will choose your next incarnation. You will likely choose to reincarnate along the same timeline as your friends and loved ones and even "enemies", but adopting a different role in this new life (a change of sex, perhaps) for further development and to work out past issues. Since you originally chose reincarnation as a tool for growth you must continue in this manner until the cycle of reincarnating has been completed (i.e., return again and again to Earth until the dense body can be shed for good), after which other methods of self-growth can be considered (choosing an all-new system of reality to experience and explore). *The fun continues!*

"Death is not real, even in the Relative sense – it is but Birth to a new life – and You shall go on, and on, and on, to higher and still higher planes of life, for aeons upon aeons of time." – the Three Initiates, *The Kybalion*

Out-of-Body Predicaments

I love all of my out-of-body experiences, even the troublesome ones. If you're out of body and conscious, it's all good. Any paranormal experience is worthwhile. However, some experiences are more daunting and irksome than others. A few even truly frightening (only because I tend to overreact). Here is a list of some of the basic problems and annoyances and intensely surprising situations I encountered while being out of body (a few of these should not be classified as problems or hindrances as they can be advantageous towards your OB endeavors, such as sleep paralysis and the vibrational state phenomena).

1. No Vision (Fear of Seeing)

In my earlier experiences, right before I rolled out of body, I'd make the mental commandment not to see anything. I had a fear that having too much visual data would scare me back into my body. Even though I had sight in my first OBE and there was nothing out of the ordinary save for some fog (my room looked as it should have), I still worried that in subsequent projections something might spook me or be so strange that I couldn't mentally handle it. If the Other Side was teeming with life right inside my own bedroom, I wouldn't be able to stay calm and the OBE would abruptly end. So I would roll out of body and walk around with no sight, arms out stretched like the Monster in *Frankenstein*.

As silly as it seems, having no vision did have a calming effect on me (like an ostrich with his head stuck in the sand). I did the "no seeing" thing for a few OBEs before I decided I was being ridiculous and needed to man up. Now what? How do I see? I'm a slow learner. It took a while to realize that I needed to either go through the motion of actually opening my etheric body's eyelids in order to see (not inherently necessary, of course, as it is only a preprogramed idea carried over from the physical plane), or to make the commandment to see. Sometimes it would work, sometimes not. Sometimes I'd think: *Screw sight,* and just do without as usual. Therefore, to save yourself the trouble it is best to be brave before slipping out of body and to not make any such "I don't want to see anything" request. For whatever reason it can be hard to gain sight once you have made a prior decision to not have it (overriding a previous commandment can be tricky – perhaps in these cases my desire to have sight was not as strong as my desire to not have it). Aside from the occasional dead pet, my bedroom was not teeming with life. In only a few experiences did I find strangers in my room and they all ignored me.

2. The Ectoplasmic Fog

This is fairly common when you first slip out of body. There is often a foggy effect, which is perhaps due to the etheric gunk or ectoplasm stirring about. I really don't know for sure what causes it or what it is. Could the fog be the lifeforce energy (or *prana*) being drawn "down" through the higher bodies into the etheric body's chakra system (raw energy being processed / absorbed)? During sleep this cosmic energy is said to flow abundantly to the etheric body (which is also known as the vital body) in order to cleanse the physical body and keep it functioning properly.

Or, perhaps, by merely shifting my etheric body a few feet away from my physical body (rolling out), I am causing ectoplasmic emanations to occur and thus creating this fog effect or mist that surrounds me, as though stirring up sediments from a seabed (stray etheric matter not yet gathered or adhering to my etheric form).

I'm likely wrong on both accounts. Whatever the case, if I move farther away from my physical body my vision will usually clear up. I have a digital clock on my night table with bright red numbers. When I go out of body sometimes my vision is so enshrouded that I have to stick my face right up against the clock to see the numbers. Other times I can see clearly in my room. You can make the statement "I now have perfect vision" and see if that helps. If not, move into the next room or go outside and your vision should clear up.

3. Reversed Vision

This has happened a few times. An example: I was living on the coast and I hadn't seen my parents for a while (they were about 100 miles inland, still living at my childhood home). Missing them, I projected just before dawn and paid them a visit (I did not have to fly the distance, as I was able to arrive there instantaneously which is not always an easy feat for me). As I reached their bedroom, I noticed that they were sleeping on the opposite sides of the bed (my dad always sleeps on the left side and my mother on the right, but it was reversed). In fact, the whole bedroom was reversed, as if I were looking at a mirrored version of the room. What would make this happen? And does it occur more frequently than I realize? It's possible that my vision in other projections had been reversed as well and I simply hadn't noticed; and whenever I had encountered a new or unfamiliar location, everything could have actually been reversed and I would not have known it (I'd just assume that everything was in its right place). However, I do know that the majority of my OBEs (that are in familiar places) did not have this issue as I can remember the layout of these experiences and everything had been as it should have been (as far as not having that mirrored effect).

So, what is the cause of this? According to Charles Leadbeater, in the book *The Other Side of Death*, this viewpoint reversal "… is an example of the confusion which so frequently occurs in the earlier experiences of the seer, before he is accustomed to the astral vision which sees from both sides at once." It is true that while projected one sometimes experiences a 360 degree vision, and apparently when looking behind oneself without turning around it can create this mirrored effect. Seems logical, although I don't recall doing this in the aforementioned example in my parents' room (or in the other examples I have). Nonetheless, I recommend that you read Robert Bruce's online article "Treatise on Astral Projection" which explains this phenomenon in much more depth.

4. Stuck In Stuff (Windows, Ceilings, Etc.)

The first time that I got stuck within an object was when I was halfway through a window (the "glass" actually bowed outward with me like bubble gum). I didn't quite get to full panic because I was able to squeeze through it with some effort. This has happened to me on more than one occasion. I tend to avoid windows now (partly because of the weird bubble phenomenon) and just walk through walls or doors or go through the ceiling; however, the *I'm-getting-stuck!* sensation can occur here as well. For example, I once floated straight up from my bed until my head was softly bouncing against the ceiling. I decided to try and push through it and was getting a lot of resistance. About halfway through it I felt as though I was getting stuck and had to back out. Perhaps the "getting stuck" sensation was partly or entirely of my creation, because of fear, of me getting trapped. Or perhaps my subtle body was more dense on these occasions. However, I think it all comes down to the rate of one's movement through an object. It appears that the slower you go through something the more likely it will feel as though you are getting stuck, because of the resistance.

Therefore, during your first OBEs it is probably best to go through objects fairly quickly so as to not create any scary (although innocuous) situations as these. Then again, you may want to experience the feeling of getting stuck. It is one of the strangest sensations, to feel matter holding onto you as you try to move yourself through it. Since most of the time you will be moving quickly, such as when flying, you will be passing straight through objects without scarcely noticing. I have yet to smack into an object when flying about. If you too have this fear of hitting something, you can try the flying backwards technique to help you get over this.

If you don't encounter the *I'm-getting-stuck* sensation, you may just get claustrophobic in some situations and panic. Diving headlong into the earth seemed like a good idea until I was down there. Surprisingly I was able to see, but being surrounded by dirt / clay and a tree root was too much like being buried alive. I could actually hear water trickling (perhaps I was in a spring water table). Even though in this experience I didn't feel matter pushing at me or squeezing me, I started to wonder if I would get stuck down here and promptly shot back out.

Since you can condense your subtle body into nothingness and enter into the smallest of spaces, other claustrophobic moments may arise, such as jumping into a pop bottle or small container and then feeling as though you are a Genie trapped in a magic lantern. However, these are all activities you should undertake if only to dispel fears. It helps to know that every situation you get yourself into is never dire – an escape route is always available, and once this is understood you will be less likely to cut a trip short.

5. Stuck In "Mud"

This is bad. One of the most frustrating things that can occur and it happens to me quite a bit, even now. It was sort of fun for the first few times but it gets old quickly. Basically, you go out of body and you can barely walk. It's as though you are stuck in mud or on fly paper, or your legs weigh so much that you can barely – if at all – lift them. It's an absolute struggle to move a few feet forward. I'm not sure what the cause of this is, or why it happens sometimes and not other times. Perhaps it is all due to some unfortunate thought processing of mine. Or perhaps, somehow, I have managed to make my double more encumbered with etheric matter than normally. Clearly something is amiss, or I've done something differently to cause this, as mobility during an OBE is normally quick and fluid. It may just be a natural magnetic pull coming from my physical body (as Muldoon believes), but as I've said, this heaviness is not always present.

When it occurs at its worst I can't even manage to leave my room (I'm lucky to make it past the foot of my bed). With my etheric body this heavy, it doesn't seem out of the question that if someone on the physical plane were in my room right then, they just might be able to get a glimpse of me (although probably, at best, just a vague semblance or outline of me). In this state, I feel more than physical, weighted down to the floor as though gravity had increased ten-fold. When its this oppressive you can't really do much about it, just wallow in the mire. If you can manage it, try to get a good distance away from your body and see if that helps. You can also attempt to shed your etheric double in order to access your astral body, but – when you are in the midst of a struggle and mentally frustrated, it's not easy to tune into a higher frequency or shift your consciousness. Alternatively, you can try getting back into your physical body and roll out again. Probably won't help. You're basically screwed here. Tough luck, soldier. Go back to bed.

6. The Sleeping Bag Syndrome (or Mummy Madness *Again!*)

This is just as frustrating as "Stuck In Mud" but more comical. It's shows you how your thoughts can be so powerful and sometimes almost impossible to break through. I used to have this bit of trouble that would happen on cold nights when I was wrapped tightly in a blanket (or sometimes in a sleeping bag). As I rolled out of body the etheric counterpart to my blanket or sleeping bag would cling to me and not let go. There I would be, on the floor, and *tightly* wound in this blanket from hell. I would be so tightly wound that I could not get up, as though I were mummified or wrapped like a moth in a cocoon. I'd try repeatedly to stand but usually no go. Sometimes I'd just give up and do the inch worm thing for a while. At those times when I was somehow able to get up, I'd just *hop hop hop* like a stupid bunny. I'd usually be laughing during all of this but it is one of my hardest thought patterns to break (I have not read of another projector having this particular problem). However, the cure for this was simple – keep the room warm (68 degrees or so). If I'm warm, then I simply won't have that incredible mental bond with my blanket or sleeping bag when I shift out of body. As long as I was snug and comfortable, there would be no thoughts of being cold tucked away into my subconscious. Thus, I am free to move about, completely unencumbered by any silly mental attachments.

7. Catalepsy / Sleep Paralysis

I've touched on this earlier in the "Questions & Answers" chapter but it deserves a few more words. Catalepsy is where you can't wake up physically. For me, this was definitely one of the most frightening things to happen to me. I had been under the assumption that if I were conscious while asleep I would be able to arouse my physical body whenever I so desired, easily and instantly, but this isn't always the case. The first time you experience this cataleptic condition is the worst, of course, but later you'll learn not to panic and actually appreciate it, as this physical incapacitation is what you want for an easy projection.

You may become aware of catalepsy or sleep paralysis while in the hypnagogic state (falling asleep) or in the hypnopompic state (waking up). During your OB practice your goal is to maintain the mind awake / body asleep mode while in either of these two states. Sleep paralysis is simply this – your body is asleep, your mind is awake, and any signal you give to your body to wake up is not being relayed to your brain quickly enough (this is why you panic).

If you find yourself awake and yet physically incapacitated, take advantage of the situation and attempt to separate from your body. If you are coming back from an OBE and can't awaken physically, don't fall into hysterics (you will, anyway, I'm sure, at least initially). But there's truly nothing's wrong here. Your body has not died on you, although it does seem that way – when you jump into your body it refuses to move. It just lies there, like a lump. And you will scream. Like a little girl, guaranteed. You can jump in and out of body several times and nothing happens. The solution is to relax, to lie down in alignment with your corporeal self and let your consciousness dim (or you can think of your fingers or toes moving and that will also work). Soon you and your body will awaken, refreshed and ready to start a new day.

8. Crybaby Syndrome

At times you may go out of body and do something ridiculously dramatic. For example, collapse to your knees and begin crying your head off – a blubber-fest of raw emotions, likely catching you off guard. For me, it is never about sadness. In fact, the crying can quickly turn into a hilarious bout of laughing and cackling. It all seems a bit insane, doesn't it? These racking crybaby fits stem from simply being overcome by the beauty of it all, being so happy, and knowing that I'm fully awake and existing apart from my physical body despite the majority of humans saying it isn't possible. The feeling of thankfulness just swells up in me. It can hit you almost immediately, or, you can start off calmly, maybe travel around a bit, admiring the crisp, glorious landscape, and then an avalanche of ELATION hits you and you collapse, and commence with the big baby bawling.

I suppose this kind of emotion is what happens when you die violently and are surprised when your consciousness is still intact, fully operating, and you notice triumphantly that you still have a body of sorts. *I'm alive! That horrible trash-compacter accident didn't kill me after all!* One of the best reasons to leave your body is to gain the full realization that you will never blink into nonexistence, to wholly and truly get it that your body is not you, that life will never cease no matter what. Just prepare for the slaphappy crying fits and caterwauling.

9. Don't Over Do It (Unless You Want To)

You can put too much emphasis on a command and get more than you bargained for. Usually you will need minimal thought power to get the job done. For example, when you initiate the rolling out of the body method of projection, you may just keep *on* rolling ... off the bed, onto the floor, through the wall or door, and into the next room or even outside. You could even keep on rolling way beyond your house if you don't get a grip and tell yourself to stop. Of course, if you enjoy rolling rather than walking or flying, then fine, be a freak. Other overly strong commands can have you shooting out of your body like a bottle rocket and beyond the stratosphere. Spinning with too much emphasis can make you feel like a motorized spindle or drill bit. You'll learn after a while to soften your thoughts and to not put too much torque behind them.

10. Disembodied, Floating Head

This was more than a tad disturbing, mainly because my physical eyes were open, though slightly rolled up. Yes, you can sometimes see otherworldly things with your physical eyeballs (well, not really – it's actually your inner sight but it seems as though you are using your physical eyes because your eyelids are open). I've had experiences of this kind before when I was a kid (as noted in the introduction of this book). In this instance I was seeing a woman's head floating in mid-air at the end of my bed. Her head moved slowly from left to right and she never looked at me. I got the impression that she had no idea I was there. She seemed disoriented, dazed. She never said a word and I was afraid to make my presence known. Then I began to come out of the trance state and the vision faded away.

Having strangers in my room has happened a few times before. An example is the young twin girls who were sitting on my floor, wearing matching yellow-and-white-striped shirts, and their father who stood next to them; they all ignored me when I tried to speak with them. But that encounter had occurred while I was out of body. In this case (the Floating Head), my physical eyelids were open and this made it especially disturbing (and that blank expression she sported added to the unease). Perhaps what I was seeing was the empty etheric shell (or what was left of it) of a woman who had passed on, her head the last portion to "decay" and merge back into the ethers whence it came.

In the book *The Other Side of Death* by Charles Leadbeater, there is an account of an individual who had seen an apparition of this type (disembodied head). This person was awake, walking down a road during the evening when this vision was seen. According to Seth, encounters of this kind may be thought-forms or partial materializations created unknowingly by the deceased who are still drawn to earthly life (these thought-forms being only partially conscious). This may explain why the twin girls and their father ignored me.

Since this "floating head" incident, I have had additional experiences where I can see nonphysical activity with my eyelids open by having my eyes rolled slightly back into my head (I suppose that's the natural state for the eyes to be in when I'm in trance). I can move physically if I want to (my legs or arms) and still be able to see into a finer dimension as long as my eyeballs remain rolled up. I think it's possible that I could walk around a bit and still be able to see this way as long as my eyes remain in the rolled up position. Previously I had believed that while in trance, if I had moved any part of my physical body other than my eyeballs I would have quickly terminated the experience. It is true that if I move my eyes back into the normal position with my eyelids open this nonphysical viewpoint would disappear (although moving my eyes left or right with my eyelids closed doesn't affect the trance condition, such as when I'm shifting a scene in a remote viewing).

I have done this quite a few times now (seeing into another realm while my physical eyelids are open). Here is another example: Early one morning I had gained consciousness, had my eyes rolled up into my head and my eyelids were cracked open. I sat up in bed just a bit and looked out between the open slats of my mini-blinds to peer outside – what I saw was astonishingly beautiful. Everything was in *extreme hyper-vivid* mode. The universe outside my window was like a cosmic soup of activity, as if a super-bright halogen lamp was placed deep in the ocean and was illuminating all of the billions of particles, except the particles weren't swirling around but moving downward at a 45 degree angle. I have not seen anything like this before, in any of my OBEs – this lovely slow-moving rain of illuminated particles, right outside my window!

An interesting tidbit: I only saw these particles when peering outside; these particles were not in the room with me (or at least I couldn't see them) – my room appeared normal in every way, but immediately beyond the glass of my window this incredible scene was occurring. I think perhaps I was having a dual plane vision, somehow able to see both the etheric (my bedroom) and the astral (beyond the window). Transitioning from one plane to another can be as easy as walking through a doorway, for example, or simply moving away from the body may trigger a plane shift. Thus, it may be possible to view another plane by simply peering through a window, similar to when I look through that small third-eye hole in some remote viewings. Also, this lighted particle experience is much different than the stars I see when looking through my eyelids in trance (i.e. the stars do not move), which I'll discuss in more detail later.

11. Malicious Spirits & Mischief-Makers

Unfortunately, there are unpleasant individuals and troublemakers on the Other Side, just like on earth. As a rule, like attracts like ... so I guess that says a lot about me, eh? Actually, I've encountered very few nasty beings; almost nil when considering the amount of projections I've had. I did have some guy screaming bloody murder at me (in a foreign tongue that I didn't recognize); I have no idea what I did to upset him. Of course I jumped right back into my body as I was too chicken to confront him. I was still wanting to leave my body again that morning but decided against it (I feared he remained at the threshold, waiting, ready to pounce).

Another unsettling experience was this: It was early morning and a couple of dead kids were horseplaying in my room, squealing and squawking, where eventually one of them kicked me in my back (or jumped on my back) while I lay in bed. I was pretending to be asleep (my mind was fully awake but my body asleep). I was still in alignment with my physical body as I had not yet separated. These two mischievous boys assumed that I was just another slumberous human. I felt they were discarnates because how at ease they were in this environment, how active and aware they were of their own selves as well as myself.

They came closer to my bed, giggling and whispering conspiratorially to each other. Now they were discussing doing something to the mini-blinds on my window. "See that string in the window? Let's untie it!" the older boy said. The little one squealed in delight, as if it were a great idea.

I never once tried to sneak a glance at them but I was able to get a sense of their ages from the sound of their very young voices. These kids weren't bad or evil, of course, just a little ornery. I was a bit scared at the moment, however, so I didn't move an inch or say anything. Afterwards I'd wished I had gotten up and chased them around for a while – I shouldn't have let them frighten me. But in the moment, when you are in stark reality, and the fact is clear that there are actually two little hyperactive imps (some might say *poltergeists*) moving around your bed and one even kicking you, it is easy to wimp-out. Today, however, I wouldn't have been so spineless – I would've tried to have a little chat with them and ask them their names.

I've had a few other experiences that were even more disquieting than the above, mainly because of the bizarre and illogical nature of them and the dark undertone. One of the worst that really scared the nonphysical crap out of me was finding a distorted clown's face on my bed (only the face, no head, resembling a stiff pancake). It was there as soon as I had projected. The worst part was that it was animated, the face bouncing left to right on my bed like some grotesque demonic wind-up toy. I just stood there looking at it, dumbstruck. I didn't understand what I was seeing or why it was here. Then the flipping action of the clown's face revved up, became more manic, and thus spooking me to where I was suddenly yanked back into my body. I immediately looked up and down my bed to make sure that that deranged clown face was no longer with me!

The interesting thing about the above experience is that while projected I could not see my physical body on the bed. This was the first time I noticed this in any OBE, to see an empty bed where my physical body should have been. I surmise the reason for this was because I was actually attuned to the astral plane (not the etheric plane) and the bed was empty because I was currently using my astral body in which to get around. It also makes sense that I was in the astral because of the clown face on my bed (this sort of abstract, insane materialization is not what you would encounter while etherically attuned – in my experience, the etheric environment is not prone to lively, psychological outbursts – but in the astral it would be perfectly natural). The reason I can see my physical body while in the etheric plane is because the etheric plane is the uppermost part of the physical plane, allowing a physical viewpoint of my body whilst my etheric body is being occupied by me in which to move about.

The above spooky examples are really about the worst I've experienced. I hope I haven't unnerved you too much by sharing them, but they really weren't that bad. The point is, these frightful experiences were basically me overreacting to innocent situations. And the really bizarre episodes (like the clown) were most likely manufactured by my psyche – free to express itself and just letting loose.

But even if something were independent of my psyche and had decided it wanted to rumble with me, I would have been safe. Again, if you become distressed over anything at all you can easily return to your body and wake up with just the thought to do so, or the heightened emotions you express (of wanting to get away or in need of help) will draw you right back in. No being can really harm you, and they certainly can't kill you. Even when that kid kicked me it didn't hurt (although I could still feel an impression on my back when I got up that morning). I don't think he was even trying to hurt me, just trying to get my attention or get a reaction from me.

The only problem with these type of experiences would be psychological. If an OBE was overly frightening to you it may prevent any subsequent conscious projections because a part of you may hold back. In this case you would have to work on your beliefs again, reaffirm to yourself that no harm can come to you as you would be within a *non-physical* state.

12. My Trips to the Moon (In-Flight Failures)

I have been trying forever to land on the moon. You would think I could just visualize myself *being* on the moon and I would be there. Not me. When I think of myself being on the moon my second body decides every time to take the long route, to actually *fly* there. I cannot for the life of me just appear instantaneously on the moon. So, I fly, higher and higher, and it is beyond beautiful every time, up and up I go, and inevitably this happens: my physical body begins to hyper-ventilate. I have dual or double consciousness – that is, I am fully con-scious as I hurtle towards the moon while simultaneously aware that my physical body is freaking out. Not just aware of it, but I can see it happening. My physical body is desper-ately fighting to catch a breath and is actually heaving. The moon's magnificence and me being so high off the ground is just overwhelming to me and my body reacts to this every time. So, after a while of this, as I physically gasp away, and

me being the big baby that I am, I finally agree with the panicky notion that I should head back home – and, of course, I have no prob-lem with getting immediately back inside my body! I can go to my body in a *flash*, sure, but not to the moon.

I would be interested to know if anyone has been able to success-fully land on the moon during an OBE (while fully conscious*).* I have some sort of rigorous mental block here. I don't have a fear of heights in physical life, and I don't usually while out of body, but I guess I just hit a point of being a little *too* high and I panic.

For me to hyperventilate during these projections should give you an idea about the reality of these experiences and how far removed from dreams they are. I have never hyperventilated in any dream before, not even a lucid dream. I, in my etheric body, fully conscious, was literally flying to the moon (the moon's etheric counterpart, anyway). Imagine that you, right now, in your physical body, suddenly rose from your chair, broke through your roof, and began to fly at a dizzying speed towards that big lunar blob in the sky. I suspect you would be wide-eyed and shaking with fear. You would probably hyperventilate as I do. There would be little difference between my experience and yours, except that I had been using a different type of body than you (and you would be headed for a certain death). Even knowing that my death was not part of the equation, when you are in the moment – much like being on a frightening yet harmless carnival ride – the freak-out quotient will go off the chart nonetheless as the danger still feels palpable. Everything around me was as real as on the physical plane – there were no dream elements or anomalies that I noticed, just stark reality in every way. Taking trips to the moon or other planets or across the universe is no problem when you are semi-conscious or dreaming – but when you do it while fully awake, when your consciousness is as bright and aware as in regular life (or more so), then it is a completely different ball game. This is why I hyperventilate. This is why I can't muster the courage to reach it. It's too real, too beautiful, and I simply can't handle it.

13. Double Consciousness

I had given an example of this phenomenon above. It is often referred to as dual or double consciousness but it should really be described as having dual channels of awareness with a single consciousness. When this occurs (and of its own volition, by subconscious direction) I am aware of two different locales (the other locale always being of my physical body). This dual awareness transpires most often when I'm in the middle of some chaotic event and I attempt to overcome my distress, trying to convince my subconscious that I want to remain outside my body despite my extreme anxiety. A sort of battle of the wills ensues. For example, my subconscious will show me (in one channel) that my physical body is uncomfortable or is having a problem and needs assistance. This is a full-on visual display of my physical body and whatever experience it is currently enduring (such as having trouble breathing). In another channel, it is me focused on whatever circumstance or task currently at hand (such as trying to get to the moon). This dual awareness occurs because of my pig-headedness to forge onward when I'm clearly not up to the challenge (my subconscious wants to reel me in but I keep insisting that I can handle it, when I clearly can't).

14. Pre / During / Post Projection Noises

Prior to leaving the body, and during the actual separation, there is quite an assortment of noises you will likely encounter and these may frighten you at first until you get used to them. I have heard buzzing; whooshing, rushing, roaring (heard while experiencing vibrations); explosion or bird squawking (heard while exiting in Spiral or Catapult Projections; an explosion sound can also occur during reentry); a chime being struck twice *ding! ding!* (this sound occurred each time that I would start to lose consciousness during my earlier OB practice; I think I had a guide trying to assist me in maintaining awareness); knocking, as if on wood; snoring (this is actually my physical body snoring; if not snoring, you may hear yourself breathing – body sounds are magnified while in the hypnagogic / hypnopompic state); thumping (heart beat magnified); my name being called (so loud it almost makes me jump out of bed); voices (people conversing with each other, nothing to do with me or about me, usually, just me tuning in to them); gunshot (always just one shot, never a round of gunfire); thought packets (not sound, just a passing of thought sent to me from another – an example is: *Have you ever heard of the phrase: Letting one's shadow know?* which was dropped into my head from an anonymous being; perhaps "shadow" being my physical waking self or ego, to "know" about my higher or whole self); cricket sounds (which I hear when meditating or concentrating at my third-eye area or the crown of my head). Some hear a click sound as they leave the body but I haven't experienced that, nor have I felt "electricity" coursing through me which is often reported in OBE literature to describe the vibrational state (rather, I would describe this state as intense waves of energy rocking and pummeling me, as though I were a small boat caught in rough waters).

Something as simple as hearing yourself snoring will tell you the obvious: that your body is asleep and your mind is awake. As you deepen this state further, the snoring noise will fade (although you may hear other sounds) and you may begin to see through your closed eyelids (seeing pinpricks of light or a starry effect, or you may begin to remote view). At this point your subtle body is now "unhinged" from your physical body and separation is possible. You may again hear body noises (snoring, breathing) on return to the body as you pass through the hypnopompic state while you begin to awaken physically (normally, however, the return to the body will not have been consciously initiated – you will be slammed back into it by your subconscious so quickly, for whatever reason, and awaken immediately that you won't hear those sounds). When dual consciousness is in effect, you can be a great distance away from your body and yet still hear the sounds emitting from it.

Conditioning / programming your body to remain asleep while you gain awareness in the morning is not as difficult as it may seem. Once you accomplish it, it will happen more and more frequently as long as you continue to reinforce your desire for the condition (via affirmations each night while you lie in bed). The most difficult part, however, is to not arouse your sleeping body when you begin to hear noises, many of which are incredibly loud. This is part of your conditioning and it takes time. It is beyond frustrating to get into the mind awake / body asleep mode only to have a noise shock you out of it. This has happened to me on numerous occasions. For example, I was once lying in bed, on my back, managed to get into the mind awake / body asleep mode and was immediately terror-strickened because of what sounded like a wild animal attacking me. I physically woke up, arms flailing at my face as I'd thought perhaps a bobcat had jumped in through my open window and onto my head (I live in the woods). But as it turned out, the noise – this frothy feral cat sound – was only me snoring!

Even if you don't snore yourself (which I rarely do), just the sound of yourself breathing can be startling. In this state even the most minute body noise can become thunderous, amplified, as though it were being played through a high-definition stereo or headset. It is really surprising how loud it can be. Once a familiarity of these sounds is established you will then be able to take control of this trance-like state and move onto the next step. With practice (as you get used to these various noises) you will discover that these sounds will awaken you without disturbing your sleeping body. In essence, you will have turned these annoying sounds into a trance aid. You will be fully cognizant (aware of who you are and where you are at). As I stated earlier, after further deepening, along with having the proper mental fortitude (i.e., lack of fear and timidity), separation from the body can then be accomplished.

15. Good Vibrations

They really are good, and nothing to be alarmed about. But, you will be alarmed the first few times! It's one of the strangest things you can ever experience. This vibrational state is thought to be a reaction of the subtle body as it begins to release itself from the physical body. You have caught yourself / become aware in the midst of this transition. However, when the vibrational state is as turbulent as I have experienced it, I can't imagine that this is due to simply the subtle body loosening its grip on the physical. I think there is much more going on here than only that, perhaps a connection to kundalini and chakra activation. There is an enormous amount of energy being released, awakening. Since we leave our bodies naturally every night, I can't conceive of vibrations this strong occurring each time while we are asleep and unaware. Rather, I believe that these type of vibrations are something a beginner experiences mostly, a sort of energy expansion or activation as one practices to consciously leave the body, like booting up a new computer for the first time.

In my experience and what I have read of others, the vibrational state becomes less likely to occur as you become more proficient at consciously projecting. However, this doesn't mean that a beginner must experience the vibrational state before he can project. I didn't have any vibrations with my first OBE (I simply rolled out of body). I don't think the vibrational state of this magnitude is a constant for anyone (it comes and goes, and becomes more and more rare as time goes on). For most of my projections I didn't experience the vibrations at all and could easily separate as long as I was in the mind awake / body asleep condition. Thus, your goal should not be focused on getting to the vibrational state but rather to condition your mind to awaken while your body is asleep. If you do experience vibrations, then go with it, but don't spend all of your effort trying to reach this state. If it does develop, be grateful, as you are bound to have an OBE if you play your cards right.

As there is some confusion from beginners to what the vibrational state actually feels like (some imagine it to be a mere shivering sensation), I will describe it in several different ways so that you will have a more concrete idea of what you may expect, although you should allow for some aberrations of your own, of course, as everyone does not experience this phenomenon exactly the same way.

At its most severe, it may seem as though you are in the midst of a powerful earthquake. The vibrations can be so rough and ragged (side to side, or up and down) that you may wonder if you'll be physically tossed out of bed (if you've seen the movie *The Exorcist* where the bed begins to bounce off the floor, that's what it can feel like as far as intensity). It will seem as though it is a physical sensation but it is the subtle body that is vibrating.

If you were conscious from the beginning of the process, the vibrations may at first arrive as a faint energy wave or a soft rocking from left to right and then, if all goes well, progress from there. Sometimes I will suddenly gain consciousness as the rocking sensation is at or near its most intense point, as though it were so powerful it had stirred me into full wakefulness. If you experience it like this (awakening spontaneously while it is happening), and you are new to the experience, then the fear you will likely express of being in the midst of a seizure-like fit would stop them almost immediately (they may, however, start up again if you remain calm and haven't moved physically). After a few episodes you will be less traumatized by these brutal awakenings and not allow trepidation or anxiety to disperse your vibrational state. When you first become aware of the vibrating / wobbling / rocking sensation, you must exude the confidence that you are okay with what is happening and wish it to continue.

Now, you may have read that the vibrations can increase to a maximum rate wherein they will have become so refined or smoothed out that, at which point, you would then be able to leave the body in whichever comfortable manner you prefer. Logically, that's how you would suppose it would work, but that's not how it goes for me. When the vibrations are at their most chaotic and coarse stage (definitely not refined), this is when I project. In fact, if I don't willfully project at this point and the vibrations continue to ratchet upwards (still far from smooth), I will be automatically launched from my body. I have categorized this manner of projecting as "Catapult Projections", which I'll describe in more detail in the "Techniques" chapter.

I seem to be the oddball here as far as exiting the body from an unrefined vibrational state. According to what I have read, it appears common that projectors leave their bodies once the vibrations have been leveled out into a much higher frequency (which makes perfect sense, but again, I don't even reach that point as I'm automatically ejected during its most chaotic stage). Perhaps this involuntary / forced projection of mine happens because of my own peculiar mindset and which may not be your experience as I have not read of others leaving the body in quite this manner. Until you get into the thick of things and see how your energy behaves, there's really no telling exactly how it will go for you.

The vibrational state may be experienced as an up and down, head to toe motion, or a left to right swaying as your subtle body goes in and out of alignment with your physical body, as though you were lying in a hammock in a gentle breeze that soon develops into a storm. Another way you may experience it (which is the most common type for me) is this: If someone stood on each side of your bed and they each, in turn, lifted one side of your body and then dropped it, back and forth, at a quicker and quicker pace. It feels as though you are a fish out of water, getting progressively more frenzied.

As I mentioned previously, Catapult Projections may be the result of my own particular mindset or energy behavior and may not occur for others. However, if you're brave enough to want to attempt this form of projection, then your job during this entire period is to encourage the vibrations to increase by pushing them along with your mind (you should have no other thought). You want to mentally fall into sync with the swaying or wave sensation and imagine it speeding up, increment by increment.

Some have taken the position that increasing the rate of the vibrations by mental impetus is not possible – that thinking (*pushing)* the vibrations to increase doesn't do anything. I maintain that it does, as it is obvious the rate of speed accelerates as soon as I "lock in" and exert my will for a quicker pace, nudging it along incrementally, persuading it to gather momentum. By doing this, however, the vibrational state doesn't smooth out or become refined, as I indicated earlier – it just gets faster and more turbulent (you are increasing the chaos). Perhaps this nudging / pushing is what causes the forced projection, to eject me automatically without my willing it. With me encouraging the vibrations in this manner – jumping ahead of the game, so to speak – I might be creating a sort of friction that propels me out of body when it becomes too intense. As to whether or not it is dangerous, there hasn't been any negative side effects of which I am aware. I see it merely as an extreme (and fun) way of leaving the body.

So, if you wish to try it, just keep the vibrations steadily increasing and you may well have an OBE without even willing the separation (as long as you don't add fear to the equation). You want to have a mind-set of calm exuberance as you rock the "boat" to its tipping point. At the precise moment that you are propelled out of body you will likely hear a loud noise, commonly described as a pop or click sound, but for me it's a bang / explosion or a bird-squawking type noise. I suspect your first Catapult Projection will be a short one, as fear will likely take over within moments of exiting. Next time, however, you will be much better prepared. I will explain how to encourage a Catapult Projection a bit more in the "Techniques" chapter.

16. The Art of Locomotion

As a neophyte to out-of-body travel, nonphysical life can be embarrassing. The most mundane things, such as walking, can sometimes cause me a bit of befuddlement. Having gotten progressively better at moving about, I can still get locked into some mobility dilemma that can be hard to break from, like a car parked into a tight spot and unable to turn itself around. You feel like an idiot, as though you are the only one who can't figure it out, and that everyone might be watching and having a good laugh. Flying, jumping, landing, going where I intend to … the OBE books I've read make nonphysical locomotion seem effortless, as though it were a non-issue.

As before stated, I have a knack for creating problems where none should exist. When fully conscious, instead of functioning intuitively (as one does in dreams), I tend to overanalyze every situation – I think too much about it – and thus create the problems. For example, walking up an embankment became quite an ordeal. Because of the steep incline, the thought occurs to me as I get closer to the top that I might start sliding – and so I do. I slide all of the way back down to the bottom. I try again. Even though I understood I was creating the situation I couldn't figure out how to stop the backwards slide whenever I neared the top. Every time, just as I would almost make it, I'd have a mental breakdown of sorts, doubting myself, and then the ridiculous slide to the bottom would happen again. The only thing I had going for me was my bullheaded determination. I kept at it, and eventually I was able to get into the correct mindset / belief that I would make it to the top and I did! I was perched on a cliff; the view from this height was fairly dramatic. Full of confidence and exuberance, I jumped off the cliff headfirst, a sort of victory dive for having reached the top and having won the battle over limiting beliefs.

Another time I had projected to my parents' house (having success-fully used the instantaneous method of travel). However, I was having major difficulty moving further. I was hovering a few inches above the ferns that grew wild along the edge of the porch. I was standing straight-up, legs moving back and forth as I tried to gain traction, arms swinging with every stride, but I remained completely stationary. It was as though a giant were holding me up by the scruff of my neck as I ran in place. My feet simply glided across this invisible ice-like sur-face. Now I was getting concerned as this had gone on for a while and I was making no progress. It was all the more frustrating because I knew my parents were nearby -- *just a few feet away* – and I was really wanting to see them. Then, abruptly, I was back in my body, having reached, I suppose, my limits of frustration and edging towards freak-out mode.

If you do encounter similar problems as these, it will likely be primarily with your first few OBEs, although it will probably happen during later projections as well (if you have a relapse in what you have learned, or lose confidence). Having your critical faculties intact can be detrimental in this regard as you will need to develop a flair for moving intuitively and not intellectually. You don't want to overthink and overanalyze every action you make or allow doubts to enter your mind, as that is akin to throwing a stick in the cog of your natural, in-stinctive abilities or senses. It's like that old cartoon with Wile E. Coyote when he runs off a cliff but doesn't fall immediately (just hovers in mid-air) *until* the moment he looks down and sees that there is no ground beneath him – then he drops. In other words, you will be productive in this "new" environment as long as you don't overlay it with doubts, or your presumptive thoughts or assumptions (mixing what you know about physical reality – such as gravity – with this reality). If you think you will fall in mid-flight, you will. If you think something may be slippery, it will be. Move about with your intrinsic knowledge, your intuitive awareness, not with your physically-centric belief system.

That being said, oftentimes a dilemma will occur not necessarily because of my overthinking but rather because I'm inherently weird. I'll create a ridiculous situation where I'm unable to break a spell that I somehow cast upon myself (such as those crazy episodes with my sleeping bag and blankets as I had related earlier). Similarly, you will probably stumble into silly situations at times that you can't easily resolve but that just comes with the territory and the psyche you have to deal with.

Flying can offer you fresh new problems. When you take flight for the first few times you may want to keep a low altitude until you build up your confidence. If you lose all trust that you can stay afloat then you will drop like a stone. Crash landings are not pretty and can be almost as traumatic as an actual plane crash, although your OBE will end abruptly as you are yanked violently back into your body. During an early OBE (at Hawaii), I would skim over the landscape not only for the great scenery but because I felt safer doing so (as opposed to being higher off the ground). As I became bold enough, I'd fly straight over a cliff and above the ocean with no worries and no crashing. You have to learn that proper thinking is your only savior. Thus, a courageous, high-spirited disposition will keep you airborne; a spineless, lily-livered inclination will drop you with no remorse.

Moving around while out of body is similar to how I "shift the scene" in remote viewings (by issuing a clear mental commandment). There is, of course, no actual need to move any of your subtle body's appendages. You don't need legs to move yourself, and you certainly don't need to flap your arms to fly. You can move forward or backward or in any direction by simply willing it (and at any speed that you want), but your thoughts must be unencumbered. This is where you learn the difference between thinking (pure intention) and overthinking (doubting, indecisiveness, apprehensiveness). Locomotion is a skill, and if you want to maneuver effectively you must zero in cleanly on what it is that you want (which direction, and how fast or slow you want to go; or to which place or person, if you desire the instantaneous method of travel), while expressing no timidity, lack of confidence, or chickenheartedness. Empty your mind and make your commandment. No need to theorize or speculate over every little aspect. Don't overthink it, just *move,* or you may end up with a completely unintended consequence, which has certainly been an ongoing problem for me (an inability to get the desired result every time). With continued practice, however, I'm sure there will be a point where out-of-body locomotion (while fully conscious) will be as intuitive and effortless as breathing is for the physical body.

You would do well, then, to take time out specifically to practice all of your different modes of locomotion, perhaps in an open field or park area. You can start off by attempting a gentle lift-off, straight up about ten feet or so from the ground, and then come softly down again. Do this repeatedly, getting a little higher each time, acknowledging how a clean commandment gives you a clean result. As you progress you can try a somersault or backflip, a mid-air twirl, or practice your rubberband man skills and the art of swinging to and fro.

I used to have fun zooming in quickly at a house or some building and stopping to study a small detail, then swinging back again to where I had started, feeling as though I were a made of rubber with an infinite stretching ability, then zooming back out again to look at another specific detail on another building. Once near a barn, speeding up to it in one grand motion and passing through a knothole with no hesitancy or second-guessing and then back out again, smooth as silk. Or diving from a tall city building for the simple thrill of it, or jumping from the apex of a house roof into trees. Or standing atop a telephone pole, surveying my exquisite domain, then taking flight again like a joyful sparrow.

Flying is what you'll be doing most often and can be the trickiest thing to master as one's fear of heights can get in the way (although this is not much of an issue for me unless I get too high). At times you'll discover that your mind is "in the zone" and locomotion control is ridiculously easy – but then I'll have a relapse and it becomes a slap-stick comedy again (a battle with my thoughts until I either prevail or my body summons me back). However, I can't complain. Every experience, no matter how frustrating has something new to offer, a new glimmer of insight of one sort or another. It's a learning process. If something doesn't work, tweak your thought processes until it does. When you're in the zone it is simply glorious. Fluidity is the word of the day. You'll be jumping from rooftop to rooftop – the distance between buildings not an issue! – the best parkour player there ever was.

To sum up this chapter: If you have experiences like these (stuck in stuff, sleep paralysis, strangers in your room, etc.), don't worry, stay calm, enjoy everything, as none of these "Out-of-Body Predicaments" are dangerous in any way.

PART TWO

Preparations / Preliminaries

Before you can consciously project, there are matters that first need to be addressed and considered. Even if you manage to get to the mind awake / body asleep stage, it won't do you much good if you can't move past the threshold and through the open "doorway". To go through, you must be able to fit – meaning, you must shrink your mental girth (fears, mainly) to an appropriate size. Since you will be conscious, getting a handle on thought control is what will enable you to move out and beyond the body for any extended period. The firmness of your mind will determine how far you will get from here. In this condition of being focused away from physical reality, the conscious ego is at first a cautious creature, like a turtle peeking out from its shell. You have left your body countless times before but to your waking self it is as though it were the first. Despite your desire, you are likely to be hesitant and halting as cowardice creeps in. Any OBEs you manage will probably be short-lived while you are adapting and acclimating to this "new" environment. After perhaps more than a few missteps, you will soon develop a hardiness, a more resolute determination that will enable you to remain outside your skin for a longer duration *so that the real fun can begin.*

Kicking the Fear Habit

If you want to have an out-of-body experience, then having the belief that OBEs are not fantasy or make-believe would help considerably. Of course, personal experience is the surest way to obtain this knowledge. But by reading extensively on the subject, talking with people you trust who have experienced it, and attending seminars and classes where OBEs can be discussed at a personal level, you can gain enough information to ascertain whether or not OBEs are valid. Also (and obviously) you must change any notions that the out-of-body experience is dangerous, unhealthy, the work of the devil, etc. Holding such beliefs are strongholds to your subconscious that you are not mentally prepared for being conscious outside your body.

Once you accept the reality of OBEs and that it is a natural and integral part of your being, the subconscious mind can now allow your ordinary waking self to experience OBEs directly – unless, however, fears are present, which then prevents the conscious mind from participating. Therefore, if you want to leave your body consciously and be in control of the situation once it has been achieved, you must first do away with the following fears:

1. Fear of separation from the physical body. You already naturally separate from your body every night as you sleep, doing various activities that you may only remember (or translate) as dreams. Much of your activity *is* dreaming. The astral realm is your natural "haunting ground", where you mastermind your most beautiful dreams and most beastly nightmares. You use dreams to communicate with yourself (regarding health issues, or possible future events or outcomes, etc.). You should be no more afraid of having an OBE than you are of dreaming, as separation from the body occurs during both.

2. Fear of the physical body dying. Your body is not going to wither and die on you just because you are away from it. It is fully able to maintain itself while you are out exploring, no matter the "distance" you travel. It has its own consciousness apart from your own. As before stated, every atom of your physical body has a singular consciousness which forms the group consciousness of each molecule, which forms the group consciousness of each cell, etc., which then forms the group consciousness of each organ, and which finally forms the body consciousness as a whole. Rest assured, your body is safely functioning whether your conscious ego is in it or not.

3. Fear of losing the physical body. We've already established that you project from your body during sleep every night even though you may not recall it, and you've made it back thus far. After all of this time, after countless projections, you have managed to find your way back home in every instance. Therefore, there's no reason to hold onto this fear. There is no chance that you are going to lose track of your body (although you may have experiences where it may seem so). Remember, whenever you want to go back to your body after a journey the "wanting" itself will reel you in.

4. Fear of the unknown. To some degree this fear will always be with you but it is well to remember that nothing can harm you out of body (laws of the physical world do not apply here), and if you encounter something "dangerous" or with malicious intent, the wish to go home – or the fearful emotion you express – will get you there. I have never experienced anything I would call truly dangerous in all of my projections – just me and my fears. It's easy to see "dangers" while out of body but most of those negative situations can be traced back to one's own psyche.

Furthermore, I think conducting elaborate safety precaution rituals before projection (which many OBE books advocate) can actually be counter-productive. By presupposing you need protection, this is creating the expectation or belief that you may encounter danger or that danger is lurking. If you are a predominantly negative person, any "white light" ritual isn't going to mask your belief system or your current spiritual DNA – you'll attract what you'll attract (based on your beliefs and the sum total of who you are presently). There is no danger, anyway – you are shifting into *nonphysical* reality. Even under the worst case scenario it is no more dangerous than a common nightmare.

If you do encounter an onslaught of unruly beings on a frequent basis, this should be a sign to you that you need to work on your everyday life – change your attitude, surround yourself with good-natured people, learn to enjoy and appreciate all of the beauty around you. Having a genuinely positive outlook during your regular waking life will certainly improve the quality of your out-of-body life.

Of course, if you are an overly fearful person it will be a challenge for you to get outside your body consciously in the first place. If you do manage it, your projections will likely be momentary until you realize that there is nothing to fear and that you are being overly cautious and worrisome for no good reason. If you can handle the dangers of physical life – where a car can run you over if you forget to look both ways – then your nonphysical life should be a breeze, as no harm can come to you.

The best way to combat fear is to confront it. Your first OBE is likely to be a quick one – out and back in again – but the next might be a little longer, and the next longer yet, for each time you make it back safely a chunk of FEAR is taken away. Be patient, practice often, and soon OBEs – like swimming – will be second nature to you.

Jonas Ridgeway

Peace & Quiet & Naked

Nothing is more exasperating than managing to get out of body only to be reeled back in because of some noise in your house that woke you up physically. Since most of my techniques require six to eight hours of sleep, this can be problematic if you are living with others. Overnight you have conditioned your body with the proper sleep and are just now preparing for lift-off, when suddenly others are getting up to make coffee and are making a racket. The remedy to this (aside from becoming a hermit) is to go to sleep a couple of hours earlier. You will then have ample time in the early morn to attempt projection before anyone gets up. Also, make sure you have your phone turned off (although it may be unlikely anyone would call you that early, just knowing your phone is on can create anxiety for you).

Another requirement is a warm environment. I like my room temperature at 68°F but this may be too cold for some. Your body needs to be moderately toasty and comfortable, preferably on your back and spread-eagle, not crunched in a tight ball trying to ward off the chill in the air. You should wear loose clothing or none at all. I don't like to wear any clothing to bed; it seems unnatural and restrictive. My birthday suit is the optimal attire. You will feel more free and unobstructed, which can only help when your goal is to exit the body. Having a warm room will also prevent those unfortunate mental attachments that I related earlier (the entanglement with my etheric blanket or sleeping bag).

In addition, I always keep a window cracked opened directly above my head to let in fresh air, even in the midst of winter (while still maintaining that comfortable 68°F in the room), but if you live in the city or a noisy area you will need to purchase some quality foam ear plugs. Having a window slightly open (preferably right above your head) is great for your health and you will sleep like a kitten – thus, you will be in the optimal mindset as soon as you start to awaken, ready to project.

91

Being healthy physically as well as emotionally is of the utmost importance. You do not want to be awake outside your body if you are feeling mentally unstable or upset over some unfortunate event in your life (if you are even able to consciously project in such a state). If so, your OBE would be chaotic / hard to control and you would likely encounter a host of quarrelsome thought-forms from the darkest corners of your psyche. It is always best to attempt projection when you are in good health and in a contented, serene state of mind.

Furthermore, you should be in a room that offers a good vibe, makes you feel the happiest and most at ease. Every room in a house has a different feel to it. You do not want to be in a room that has a negative history, where a bad argument or fight had occurred, or if the color scheme and décor puts you in a dour mood. Such a room would attach a heaviness to your psyche that would not be beneficial for projection.

Also, you should not consume too many liquids before going to bed. If you do manage to project, having a full bladder is going to be an excuse for your body to bring you back home before you are ready.

And finally, according to both Seth and Robert Monroe, lying in a north-south position with one's head to the north is advantageous. Supposedly the magnetic field helps to draw out the subtle body from the physical (I believe this idea originated with yogi masters). Although I have not personally noticed a difference by lying in this position, you may want to take this into consideration.

The good news about using my methods of projection is that there is no need to go through any body relaxation exercises. Many books spend a great deal of time explaining how to "calm" each body part from head to toe. They'll have you sit in a chair or adopt some meditative posture where you'll then begin a long and repetitious process of relaxation, and how to breathe properly. It's not that I don't think there is any merit to this way of doing it, only that I have not been successful with it. It's difficult for me to shut down my body's senses without having slept first. I simply need a few hours of sleep between me to get into the proper relaxation state (the hypnopompic state) in which to project. Since sleep as a means of relaxation works so well and doesn't take any training, I'm sure it is the best option for beginners. You will be able to focus on learning the actual art of separating from your body rather than spending time on any elaborate relaxation ritual. I will explain this further in the "Techniques" chapter.

Techniques for
Out-of-Body Travel

Whether you believe it or not, you have other bodies beyond the physical. They exist whether you accept their existence or not, and they separate from your body each night whether your outer ego is aware of it or not. The beautiful truth is, you have the power within you to direct these other bodies with your usual waking consciousness if you choose to do so. As before stated, depending upon the person and to which plane one is attuned, its appearance ranges from a near-exact replica of the physical body to a nebulous luminosity, to nothing at all but one's consciousness. Whichever way you experience it, to whichever vibratory plane you shift, it only takes one fully conscious OBE to change your life. By using the following techniques – the same ones I use – you will be able to verify for yourself that consciousness can, indeed, separate from the body and move beyond it. It will take some discipline, a lot of conditioning, but it is surprisingly doable in a relatively short amount of time.

As you can surmise, having the ability to project your consciousness can offer you many opportunities. I am still learning how to control my OBEs myself, but when you have developed your out-of-body skills enough it is possible to go nearly anywhere that pleases you. You can travel the world over (for the pure enjoyment of it, or to visit loved ones). Or even out of this world, if it suits you. To the moon, perhaps, or farther still. Or you may leave the etheric plane altogether and shift on through to the astral realms, where creativity and self-expression thrive.

Understandably, being able to do all of these things may seem a bit implausible or purely fictional to you but the truth is there are few limitations. Although I consider myself an unfocused, sloppy projector, I have had enough OBEs to satisfy myself that the only limitations are those that are self-imposed (that is, excepting those higher planes one may not yet have access to at their current stage of development). Theoretically (not confirmed by me, anyway), if one is spiritually evolved enough he can reach beyond the etheric and astral planes to even subtler realms by projecting successively from each of his lower vibratory bodies (the last two highest planes, the so-called heavenly regions, are said not to be accessible by *any* man in our current stage of evolution). In my case, I believe the upper astral plane (and perhaps the lower mental) is the "highest" I've managed thus far, with having mainly roamed the etheric plane. The fact that I'm so often earth-bound with my etheric projections makes it quite clear that I'm not yet ready to move much beyond the baby stages of being out of my skin. I'm still new to all of this, even after years of doing it.

So, without further rambling, here are the various techniques for waking one's consciousness while the body sleeps, and the methods of projecting. However, I don't see the point of listing every method known as most of them are quite similar (there are only so many ways to project one's consciousness). Many books will be generous with their various projection methods, going into great detail but also, in my opinion, making the process overly complex. Some readers may be thinking that if they keep on searching they will someday stumble upon that mythical golden method that will *finally* allow them to project. Instead, as I mentioned previously, you should focus your energy on maintaining the mind awake / body asleep state, wherein your body is in a perfect state of catalepsy or sleep paralysis. This is where your efforts should be directed, as this is the point where you will be finally able to separate (that is, if your emotional state is favorable). Nonetheless, I will still list a few other methods I have used as well, such as the following Dream-State Method.

The Dream-State Method

Although not the easiest method (and perhaps not the best method for beginners if you have a fear of flying), a good method for inducing an OBE is via the dream state. But before we go into details, we need to go over some preparatory matters.

1. You need to become obsessed with OBEs and the idea that YOU can experience them. This is important. You can't just want to leave your body, you must desire it. You should read everything of quality you can about OBEs. You should think about it every free moment that you have. Pound it into your head! Read what it feels like to go out of body, to rush at super-human speeds, to float serenely above treetops and spin dizzily with the stars – then imagine yourself doing these things. As you drift off to sleep, imagine that you are weightless, that you are floating toward the ceiling, then passing through the ceiling, through the roof, hovering above your house and then drifting peacefully over your neighborhood. Do this each night, and when you have done this for some time you will find that flying dreams are more frequent – and you are that much closer in taking control of them.

Granted, reading OBE literature indiscriminately can give you a false depiction of what the nonphysical experience is actually like and may cause you to mimic those ideas in your projections. Some books warn of dangers, of demons or foul creatures that won't let you pass certain areas or are out to cause you harm, to sap your energy, etc. These are falsehoods perpetuated by those caught up in their own hallucinations and don't recognize them as such, and then write about them. Similarly, many (if not most) of the books about the near-death experience also get entangled in their hallucinations but in a different way, such as those who report visions of heaven, angels, pearly gates, God's throne, etc. These are also mind constructions. In the latter example, these type of hallucinations (of a religious nature) can be useful for those who have actually died as they serve as a comfort while transitioning from physical to nonphysical reality. Eventually these individuals will realize the hallucinations for what they are (sometimes with the assistance of a guide / teacher, or a loved one) and can then move forward to the next stage in their development.

Although reading about leaving the body – getting emotionally excited and enthused – can definitely be an aid to having your own OBEs, and it certainly was in my case, you do run the risk of creating falsehoods by ingesting material that is inaccurate. If a book is suffused with fearful stories then you can bet the author is consumed by his own hallucinations and your reading of it may be detrimental to your projections if you take what is written as an expected condition. The best use of OBE literature in this regard is in the descriptions of separating from the body, floating, and flying, as these are generally in alignment with how most OBEers experience it. These vivid narratives can get your psyche primed – juiced up – and you will begin to dream of these very situations and sensations (flying, especially, being helpful).

When you dream of flying – in a plane or Superman style – it is, in most cases, an actual out-of-body experience (the subtle body has sep-

Jonas Ridgeway

arated from the physical body but instead of being controlled by the conscious mind, it is in the process of performing the scene or dream that the subconscious mind has created). Thus, when you dream of flying, you usually *are* flying. Furthermore, flying in a dream isn't the only time you're out of the body while dreaming. Indeed, most if not all of your dreams – even the mundane, boring ones – take place away from the physical body.

And what of those curious falling dreams? We have all experienced them, the sensation of falling and then waking with a sudden jolt or jerk. This is what occurs when the subtle body is called back too abruptly, as it makes a quick descent (the falling sensation) and then reenters the physical body (the sudden jolt). While projected, rarely will you return to your body in a civilized manner, certainly not when fear is a factor – you'll be propelled backwards and essentially body-slammed into it. Even if you were only mildly afraid of something and not ready to go back yet, the forced return to your body can be brisk and brutal (although painless). You can sometimes override fear with sheer willpower as your subconscious becomes more flexible but it is not easy.

I say that being pulled back into one's body is painless, and it is, but I have read reports to the contrary. I think in these cases the individuals are confusing pain with that of sensation. You may feel a lingering mental discomfort or pressure after a forced return but it certainly cannot be described as pain in any sense of the word (at least in my experience).

When the goal is to stay out as long as possible, returning to your body will not be of your own conscious volition – it will be your subconscious that decides to end your trip (be it a loud noise, or some physical body issue it wants you to attend to, or, of course, if you are exhibiting fear). As you are yanked back into your body it is, as I've said, almost always quite jarring and you will immediately awaken. On the other hand, you do always have the choice to return to your body on your own and reenter it gently (as long as you don't mind cutting your playtime short). All that is needed is for you to lie down in alignment with your physical body and let your consciousness dim. In my case, however, in those rare occasions when I do decide to return on purpose, a clumsy, ungraceful reentry is usually the norm – I tend to crash into my nest like a dim-witted bird! This inelegance is mostly due to laziness and a desire for a quick wake up.

2. In order to bring the dream state in view, you must remember your dreams – which brings us to Dream Recall. By keeping a record of your inner self's activities, it will allow you to see the patterns and connections between them.

First, a healthy body with optimal levels of vitamin B6 and zinc supposedly helps to register one's sleep activity (dreams, OBEs, spirit conversations or messages) to the brain upon waking, as does lying in a north-south position with one's head to the north (in addition to memory retention, the magnetic pull is thought to aid in projection itself). Abstaining from caffeine and alcohol is also believed to pro-mote recall.

Next, by recording your dreams in a journal – faithfully, and in as much detail as possible – the act itself will help you recall them better and more often. Dreams are rather slippery, so keep your journal next to your bed with pen handy and write them down immediately upon waking. Record everything you can remember, even if only a bare whisper remains (something seemingly insignificant may jog your memory as you write it down). If you have symbols or strange objects in your dreams, draw them out as best you can while writing a description as well. All of your dreams are valuable and have merit, so honor them by having a permanent record of them.

3. Suggestions / Affirmations before going to sleep – especially as you drift off to sleep – can be extremely effective. I will give you a few examples later on in this chapter that you may use.

I will now go into the added benefits that projection via the dream state offers over other methods. First, the element of fear in relation to the separation from the physical body isn't present as when the trance condition is used. When consciousness is brought to a dream – which is the crux of the experiment – the physical body has long been side-lined, so to speak, and therefore separation anxiety is not an issue (by the time you have gained your awareness separation has already taken place). On the other hand, if you get fearful about something in the trance state (as in feeling the subtle body rocking / swaying, or the sensation of floating upward) you will often jar your physical body awake, ruining the experiment for the time being.

Another advantage of The Dream-State Method is this: As stated above, when you have a great interest in the subject of OBEs many of your dreams will be related to OBEs, thus giving you easy – and tailor-made – opportunities in which you can transform these dreams into OBEs. For example, I once dreamt that I was climbing this steep mountain – its characteristics and the surrounding area made me think of Peru – and because (in the dream) I was tired, I thought: *Hey, wouldn't it be great if I could go out of body and just fly up?* And with that I realized I was dreaming and took advantage of the situation, opening up my awareness and allowing for an out-of-body experience to emerge.

While bringing awareness to a dream is a crucial step in having a proper OBE, how does one go about doing this? One way is to find something in the dream that is out of place, doesn't belong, or seems too fantastic to be real. An example: I was dreaming that I was at my parents' house in their large upstairs bedroom. It was daylight in the dream (nighttime in reality) and the room looked normal save for these tall, individual mirrors that stood next to one another and surrounded the room. Although I was only partially conscious, I knew these mirrors didn't belong here (the sheer number of them was quite ridiculous, perhaps a dozen or more) and so I came to the notion that I must be dreaming. I thought: *Okay, to prove that I'm dreaming I'm going to jump out the window.* I had gotten this silly idea from Oliver Fox's book *Astral Projection* where he had jumped out of a window during a dream to prove that he was dreaming. Thus, I did just that, leaping out of the window without hesitation, but before hitting the ground I was able to lift up and commence flying. Once having realized your dreaming condition, you have "turned up" your consciousness considerably and can then take further steps to acquire your complete awareness (dispelling all dream elements so that you may continue on in the actual out-of-body environment).

Although projection via the dream state is a worthy method, once you have reached your self-awareness / self-identity, getting rid of the lingering dream aspects can be a challenge. These hallucinations may cause you a problem if you don't realize them as just that – hallucinations. Of course, if you want to play around with the hallucinations you can do so (after all, you created them). But if you wish to have an OBE that is removed from your psychological fantasies, then you must, upon viewing a suspected hallucination, tell it to go away or disappear, and it will. However, if you don't realize a hallucination for what it is you always run the risk of sliding back into a normal dream state. Therefore, you should make the statement: "I see only the real environment!" Making this statement aloud – and loudly – will also affirm to you your cognizance and assist in the stabilization of your consciousness.

Furthermore, although it may seem ridiculous, I will shake my head back and forth and "stretch" my eyes wide to help acquire additional wakefulness (think of Lon Chaney in the movie *Phantom of the Opera* and you'll get my meaning). This "eye stretching", of course, is only a psychological exercise as I have no real eyes – it's something that I do physically when I'm exhausted and trying to stay awake and it helps while OBEing as well. These are just a few of the things I do (I will list more below). Once you open yourself up to full consciousness – a super hyper awareness – any remaining dream remnants will have dispersed.

Now, once your basic awareness and I-AMness has been acknowledged, in order to turn on the total waking self you should do the following (in addition to the above): realize that while your physical body is asleep, YOU are awake; affirm that you are completely conscious and in complete control; state your full name, address, phone number, and your parents' names; do a few jumping jacks (I'm not kidding), shouting "I'M OUT OF BODY!", and then, finally, with arms akimbo, throw your head back and laugh maniacally (okay, you may skip the crazed laughing part). Yes, I actually do all of these things. The idea here is to reinforce that you have your critical faculties fully operating, kind of locking it in, so you don't slip into a regular dream mode again (which is easy to do if you're not careful). Stating your phone number, etc., really does help as it takes a bit of concentrated effort to do so and thus solidifies your alertness. At this point, you should be as attentive and cognizant as your everyday physical consciousness (or more so).

As I've experience many times, fear within a nightmare can hit one with a vengeance. However, fear in a nightmare – especially the "life-threatening" kind – can be used to your advantage with regards to full consciousness awakening. For example, I once dreamt that I was being menaced by a ghost that darted about me in an unfamiliar room. I was twirling like a madman, trying to keep my sights on it. As I ran toward the French doors with plans to crash through it, I thought: *Maybe I can pass right through it like I do in OBEs!* And with that I was able to go through it and went on to have one of my longer, completely conscious out-of-body experiences.

Thus, once a familiarity with OBEs is established (by firsthand experience or by reading) the knowledge gained will often present itself in the dream state, creating ideal opportunities in which awareness can be reached.

To avail yourself of additional opportunities of this kind, the use of affirmations is highly recommended. They can be quite potent – do not think of them as a waste of time. Affirmations are a powerful tool to program your mind with your specific desires. They can be used for many different purposes, to support your healing, overcome addictions, build confidence, etc., or for something as trivial as to awaken at a specific time (I'd often program myself to wake up at 6:30 AM just as the stock market opened, even replicating the exact ringtone of my cell phone which served as the alarm). We already use affirmations constantly in our daily lives, it's that voice in your head that's mostly negative. We pummel our selves with negative thinking and then wonder why our lives are filled with aggravations and misfortunes. You can reverse this by switching to a positive affirmation whenever you catch yourself in a negative one.

For the goal of having an OBE or to become lucid while dreaming, affirmations are used to insert these specific instructions into your subconscious mind. Accordingly, a suggestion before sleep should always be given. For the best results for dream recall, you can make the suggestion to awaken as soon as each dream has ended (as you have several dreams throughout the night). As you lie in bed repeat your affirmations several times (preferably aloud), feeling the meaning and intention of the words. Speak slowly and confidently. Here are a few examples (you may edit them as you wish to suit you):

I REMEMBER MY DREAMS

I AWAKEN AFTER EACH DREAM HAS ENDED

I AM ABLE TO HAVE A LUCID DREAM

AS I BEGIN TO DREAM, I GAIN FULL AWARENESS OF MY TRUE OUT-OF-BODY CONDITION

I AM ABLE TO HAVE A FULLY CONSCIOUS OUT-OF-BODY EXPERIENCE

An alternative approach that may prove more effective is to burn a CD or make an audio MP3 recording that repeats your affirmations / mantras (in your voice) for about 10 minutes as you drift off to sleep. It is also highly recommend that you suggest the type of dream you desire so that you will recognize it when it occurs. For example, you may suggest a dream in which you are hang-gliding over the Grand Canyon, or a seagull soaring over the breaking waves of a coastline. You should choose a flying-type dream as the sensation of flight that you experience may bring about the realization of your true condition – that you are actually out of body.

In addition, you should leave affirmations on Post-it notes throughout your home (around your computer monitor, bathroom mirror, refrigerator, etc.); these should be written in heavy block print in black ink. As you glance at these suggestions throughout the day you are reinforcing your programming. You should also repeat your affirmations aloud whenever you have free time available (showering, running, etc.). This may seem a bit overboard but all of this helps to condition your mind for some interesting activity during the night and early morning.

The Morning Method: The Easiest Method for Inducing the Out-of-Body State

The hypnagogic and hypnopompic states are stages of half-sleeping, half-waking that we pass through as we fall asleep and as we awaken. With practice, you can learn to sustain this state and elevate your wakefulness while your body remains sleeping. It is this mind awake / body asleep state that I am in when I am remote viewing – seeing through walls (which is shown as a small hole opening), "moving" down roads, or reading literature. This last I have done many times, reading poetry, pages from magazines, novels, and metaphysical books including one by Seth that doesn't, as far as I can tell, exist on the physical plane. If you don't see any actual books it may just appear as writing on the ceiling (sometimes in an unknown alphabet). Or, your ceiling may have been replaced altogether with countless stars. Symbolic imagery (as I had related earlier) may also occur. Most importantly, this state is also ideal for projecting the consciousness from the body.

My first OBE was done from this state. I had begun to waken after several hours of sleep and was seeing through my eyelids (this is not a prerequisite for an OBE but can serve as a sign that conditions are favorable for one). After the vision of my mother in the kitchen (see the chapter "My First Out-of-Body Experience"), I simply willed myself to roll off the bed to the right and instantly my wish was granted (the principle of "thought is action" is applicable while in this state, as it is while out of body).

To be clearer (as I have been asked this a few times by beginners) the process of rolling out of body is initiated in the same way if you were to roll off your bed physically – thus, by "willing myself", I simply mean the performance of the actual act. You don't need to visualize the act of rolling, you just roll. If you want to stand up, you stand up (you don't need to visualize this act, you just do it, in the same way you would if you were doing it physically). However, visualization will work as well – if you want to shoot your consciousness across the room, for example, then you would just think of that happening (a clear thought with intention) and it will.

Now, as the above example demonstrates, separating one's consciousness from the body can be achieved rather effortlessly from the mind awake / body asleep state. But now the question is, because this state is usually of short duration, how does one prolong it in order to have an OBE?

First, because OBEs are more conducive after six to eight hours of sleep, this is where you should begin (no relaxation exercises are needed because the sleep process has already taken care of that). As you feel yourself coming out of sleep do not move your physical body and keep the eyes closed. This may seem an impossibility (it does take practice) but you will soon develop the habit of remembering not to move your body as you first become cognizant. Using an affirmation before bed should be of help. The goal here, then, is to be completely self-aware but to allow your body to remain asleep. It must be asleep for you to project!

To maintain consciousness, you stare at a fixed point in front of your eyes. Keep your consciousness steady; don't allow it to drop below too many notches (if you hear your physical body snoring or shallow breathing you may go a little deeper). Try not to think about your body or you may signal it to wake up. Keep all thoughts about your physical life as far away as you can. Remain focused on basically no thought (extraneous thoughts will distract you and drag you down into dream mode). You just want to bask in this calm and peaceful state of being, right on the borderland of two realities.

At this point you may have the ability to see through your eyelids, hear voices or strange noises, feel vibrations or a rocking / swaying sensation, or none of these things – at any rate, to ascertain whether or not you are in the correct mode for an OBE, simply get up (if you are in the correct mode your physical body will not move and it will be left behind).

Most likely, however, because you undoubtedly have some amount of fear, you will experience many "shifts" before actually experiencing sustained separation from the physical body. A "shift", as I like to call it, is when you feel your consciousness shifting or moving briefly to another position outside your physical head. This separation may last only a second or two. As you become more used to the sensation of your consciousness moving, the duration of the shifts will be longer. You may, for example, now be able to sit up for a few moments. On the other hand, if you are the fearless type, perhaps complete separation can be accomplished and sustained from the onset, bypassing the shifting nuisance altogether.

Alternatively, you may be more at ease with an exaggerated slow exit: popping out an arm, a leg, the other leg, the head, etc. I prefer to exit in one nice clean swoop (no need to dawdle) but it doesn't always work that way. There has been on occasion where I needed to apply some force to get out, a bit of wiggling and stretching as though I were giving birth to myself, until I managed to break free. It is unlikely you will have this situation often, if ever (I think this type of exit is rare). If you are indeed in the mind awake / body asleep state, and you haven't let fear overpower you, then making your exit should be surprisingly easy and not involve too much nuisance.

If you find it overly difficult to not move your physical body and keep the eyes closed when you first awaken in the morning, try setting your alarm for only five hours of sleep instead (or better yet, since alarms can be too much of a jolt, or if you have a significant other that you don't want to disturb, program yourself with the suggestion to come awake at this time), then get up, go to the bathroom or walk around for a few minutes, crawl back into bed and lie on your back (being on your back is extremely important). This alternative method should help you quite a bit as you have not yet finished sleeping and are just tired enough to allow yourself to slip into that prized threshold of mind awake / body asleep. I've had many easy OBEs this way (having gotten up for a short while and then back into bed again). Plus, now that you are on your back you are in the most favorable position for projection.

Next, close your eyes and do the mental exercise of lowering yourself down to the hypnagogic state. Your body, after five or six hours of sleep, is very relaxed, making it easier for you to edge it down slowly into a comatose-like condition while your mind remains at least somewhat aware (be careful not to lose control of your consciousness or the experiment is over; this is where practice comes in).

As you change your focus away from physical reality (which will feel as though your body has disappeared) you will hit a point where you will sense that you are in the correct mode for an OBE. Besides all of the tell-tale signs described earlier (which may or may not be apparent), the correct mode, in my experience, is this great sense of utter calmness, a deep feeling as though I'm sitting peacefully at the bottom of a swimming pool. When I recognize this state I'll initiate the exit from my body.

When attempting to project from this state it is important that you do not try too hard. If you try too hard or become anxious, you will destroy any chance you may have had. Adopt the attitude that you don't care whether or not you project. You want to be casual about it, indifferent. It seems counter-productive but behaving in this manner will keep your fears at bay (the actual desire and intention to project, of course, are still there; you are only pretending, which keeps you calm). When you have determined that you are in the mind awake / body asleep state and have managed to hold that position steadily, simply initiate the act of leaving your body in whichever manner you feel most comfortable.

A good method – the one I use most often – is to roll off the bed to the right or left. Or, if you like, imagine yourself floating out (this may not be best for beginners, however, if you tend to overreact to new and bizarre sensations). Choose whichever exit method you feel is the most natural or suitable for you.

The best method is the one that can get you out of the body quickly, such as the rolling-off-the-bed method. If you choose this method, it is a good idea not to have objects in your path such as a desk or night table. Although your subtle body can *usually* pass through such objects with no resistance, despite knowing this, if you harbor fears of rolling into an object or knocking your head against something, then complete separation cannot be accomplished (having a clear path will allay any such concern).

Once out, keep it in mind that a too close proximity to the physical body might yank you back into it before you are ready. If you want to, you can look back at your physical body but the initial shock of seeing yourself with a such a deathlike, slack-jaw appearance will likely bring about reentry into your body. Your sleeping self does not look particularly attractive (at least in my case!) and it might jolt you back to physical reality. Looking at your body is certainly something you'll want to do at some point but you might want to save that experience for a subsequent projection. Whatever you do, don't think of moving any of your physical body parts as that will pull you back into your body and awaken it.

In short, separating from your body is an ultra-sensitive act. I still often go through a couple of "shifts" first before I am able to stay out for a while. After you have managed to make a complete separation, if you show fear for even a millisecond, that's all it takes – you will be sucked back into your body like a vacuum. If this happens (and it will as a beginner), you can quickly recover by making a decidedly confident, assured exit this time around. If you falter again, just keeping rolling out (or whichever exit method you use). You can have many chances at separation if you have learned to not move your physical body after each reentry. In the past I would often have a half dozen shifts or so before I was confident enough for a strong, sustained separation. However, since reentry is usually jarring, it will take some practice to have more than one separation per session.

As you become more experienced with the separation process and have managed to stay outside your body for minutes at a time, you can start to have some fun and be creative. Experiment. After performing a sitting-up separation, I'll often crawl to the end of the bed and do backflips or somersaults. If I'm really in a nutty mood I will simply think *Turn! Turn! Turn!* and my subtle body will spin at an incredible speed (like a whirlwind or that Tasmanian Devil cartoon character). Sometimes I feel so free and happy that I'll indulge in a bit of dancing, jigging across the room or in midair. A few times I've heard strangers nearby but was unable to pinpoint their location. I'm sure they found my antics quite humorous, as though they were watching an overly-hyper kitten at play.

The Catapult Projection Method

This method is a variation of the above method and is intended as the madman's approach to leaving the body – it's effect is that your subtle body will be rocket-launched from your physical body! This method uses the vibrational state as a means of projection, which I discussed earlier in the "Out of Body Predicaments" chapter. I wish to go into a bit more detail on how to induce Catapult Projections as this experience is so outrageous and unlike anything you've probably experienced before. This method is not for the squeamish. If you sincerely want to feel what it is like to be shot from a cannon, then give this method a go. I love this method, but I'm a little nuts.

Throughout my childhood I had been aware of a strange pulsing or throbbing sensation in the space in front of my closed eyelids, and to entertain myself, I'd often "watch" it, and I soon discovered that by concentrating on it the pulsing action could be sped up. I'd given the phenomenon a name – "The Whomp-Whomp Thing" – which, I thought, would describe perfectly the sound it made if it had had a sound.

Later, after my mother had told me of her OBEs and OBEs in general, I discovered that the pulsations didn't reside solely with the eyes but my entire body, and that by concentrating on the sensation (or sometimes at a point above my head, as if I were wearing an imaginary hat or cap) the pulsations would intensify and speed up; and when sped up to a point, I would begin to rock back and forth, although physically I did not move. Everyone has this inner rhythm which is simply the vibration of the subtle body – it may be so "quiet" or gentle to your senses that it goes unnoticed – but when magnified and quickened while in the mind awake / body asleep state, can unlock (*catapult!*) the subtle body from the physical.

To become aware of the vibrations of your subtle body you should be lying on your back after six to eight hours of sleep, just as you awaken. Don't move your body and keep your eyes closed. Continue to relax – drifting down carefully to that delicate state between half-awake and half-asleep.

Now look at the darkness in front of you. Is there a gentle "pulsing action" or a strobe-light effect? Can you feel the "Whomp-Whomp Thing" behind your eyes and between them? If so, imagine it speeding up or increasing. Do you feel the pulsations, as if a gentle wave of energy is undulating throughout your body? Make the pulsations stronger by following the rhythm in your mind. Imagine it speeding up, becoming more pronounced and powerful – push it along with your mind. When the pulsations have increased to a certain point, you should feel a rocking sensation from left to right as the subtle body begins to loosen itself from the physical body. Keep this sensation going by imagining it moving faster and faster. If you can continue this crazy rocking / wobbling motion without becoming frightened eventually your subtle body will be *blasted* into space!

At least, this is how it works for me. As I stated before, Catapult Projections may be an abnormality of my particular energy. I haven't read or heard about others leaving the body in this manner so it is unknown whether this out-of-body *ejection* method will work for others. All I can say is to give it a try, if you dare.

At the moment of exiting you may hear a loud noise, a high-pitched, animal-like sound or as though a bomb went off. At the beginning, however, and throughout, you may hear a rushing, roaring or whooshing sound that gets louder until separation. When separation has occurred, you will have been propelled upward to a considerable height at a roughly 45 degree angle, make an arc, and then come smoothly down (unless you decide to initiate continued flight). If this was your first Catapult Projection then you will probably be back into your body before you knew what hit you.

If you weren't catapulted, it may have, instead, sent you off like a spinning top, spiraling upward (you actually twirl forcefully as you separate). A Spiral Projection feels as though you are an out-of-control firecracker. However, with a Spiral Projection, although powerful, you will probably not be projected a great distance from your home and may even remain in your room. I don't know why sometimes I get a Spiral Projection instead of a Catapult Projection – it is sort of a crapshoot as to which will happen.

I realize this method isn't suitable for anyone but thrill-seekers. If you want an exit from the body that isn't nearly as alarming as the above, then you should just imagine your subtle self rolling off the bed in one gentle fluid motion – do this before the rocking sensation has become too extreme to prevent the forced projection. You will know when you are succeeding when you feel your consciousness withdrawing from the physical body. After complete separation has taken place, forget about your physical body and think only of how calm and relaxed you are (repeating a word, such as "peaceful", may be of help to keep your mind at ease and preoccupied). If your sight is blurry, move away from the physical body until your vision clears. If it remains blurry, will yourself to see more clearly.

The Visualization Method

These methods all use the same principle, to sort of trick your subtle body into separating from your physical by using visualization. These visualizations should be attempted as well after six to eight hours of sleep. When you first start to become cognizant, don't move your body or open your eyes and work your way back towards the mind awake / body asleep state (as explained earlier) and then maintain it.

Next, simply visualize the movement that it would take to climb either a ladder, a rope, stairs, etc. It is the movement you will be visualizing, not the object itself. This ascension should be visualized directly above you (above your consciousness). Choose the movement that appeals to you the most and feels the most natural. Success is in the details, so make your ascension as realistic as possible. I will remind you again that when you feel yourself withdrawing from your body, it is imperative that you remain calm and focused. The slightest hint of anxiety can throw you back down again. Just continue your ascent until you sense that you are a good distance away from your body or in the room above you or on the roof. You may or may not feel resistance when moving through the ceiling (for the best chance at an easy pass, do not think about resistance or you'll surely create the sense whether it is actually there or not). Variations on this theme can be an elevator, trampoline, bouncing ball (where your conscious is the ball), etc.

One especially effective method is to imagine that you are lying in a hammock that is gently swaying, and then, slowly, it begins to increase its momentum. This is a good way to fire up the vibrational state. You can also try visualizing the motion of sitting in a swing. However, with these visualizations you may accidentally trigger a Catapult Projection if the momentum hits its crescendo.

I also like the Expanding Consciousness Method, where you simply visualize that your consciousness is growing larger until it encompasses your entire bed, your room, your house, at which point you may suddenly realize that you are, indeed, actually outside your body, perhaps hovering over your home.

Finally, if you see that your ceiling has been replaced with a night sky filled with stars, you will know for a fact that you are in the correct mode for an OBE. Simply reach for the stars and you will begin to move upward and out of body.

The Portal Method

This is one of the most amazing methods I have used and the idea came about during a session of remote viewing. I was curious what would happen if I tried to actually jump into a random scene in a remote viewing. Not only is this method great for exiting the body quickly, it is also a great way to transfer your consciousness to a wildly different area than your bedroom. You will need to be proficient at remote viewing to take advantage of this method, or you can try it the next time you have an RV spontaneously.

There's not a whole lot of difference between jumping into a scene (using The Portal Method) and projecting to another location or person via a regular OBE – the main difference being that with this method the location is random (seemingly) and you'll be getting a preview of it before jumping into it. Nonetheless, it is something you should experience at least once as it is an interesting variation from a regular projection.

My first attempt at jumping into a scene was surprisingly easy. I have only used The Portal Method with wide-screen remote viewings, not those in which I am peering into a small hole or a coned / tapered vision. Not that I believe I couldn't do it with those types of visions, only that I have yet to attempt it.

To jump into a scene from a remote viewing you simply jump into the scene! Simple enough. You really only need to desire being within the scene itself while making a move towards it. Now, normally in a remote viewing when I want to move a vision forward (as though to "move" down a road, for example) I would just mentally push it forward while still remaining in my room – but this time I've added the desire to enter the scene itself and that's exactly what occurs. I go from lying prone in my bed to suddenly *whooshing* into the scene. My consciousness has been transferred to that exact location.

My first experience with The Portal Method was when I jumped into heavy traffic within an unknown city (suddenly there I was, running alongside various vehicles – and then shortly I shifted back into my room again). Another time I was on a hillside where a group of teenagers were hanging out (each wearing a different colored bomber jacket). In another I was flying through a canyon which resembled Utah, buzzing around the monoliths at an incredible speed. Unfortunately these portal jumps don't normally last long. As with a regular projection, it is easy to get alarmed about something and cut the experience short.

The X Marks-the-Spot Method

As usual, this method should be used after six to eight hours of sleep. This is the lazy man's projection technique that I came up with one morning. As you begin to awaken do not move the body and keep your eyes closed. The idea here, believe it or not, is to fall asleep again – but this time with a particular goal planted firmly in your mind as you drift off into slumberland. That goal is to fall asleep while imagining that your consciousness is positioned at a specific area on the floor somewhere in your room (X marks the spot). Just imagine yourself, that pin-point of consciousness that is YOU, is on the floor next to your bed, or near your dresser, or wherever – keep this idea firmly rooted as you fall asleep. Again, the only thing that you should be thinking is that your conscious is no longer fixed in your head but somewhere else in your room and then just relax and slip down into sleep while maintaining that laser-like intensity of thought.

This technique is simple but it works great for me. The next thing you'll be aware of is that suddenly your consciousness has fallen to the floor to that specific area, and this very act of falling, this *movement*, actually brightens or heightens your consciousness so that you clearly understand what has happened: that you are now outside your body.

The swooping motion of your consciousness is surprising when it occurs – unless you are used to the motion of shifting out, you will get pulled back into your body by just expressing the slightest moment of fear. When this happens, as it probably will, just keep repeating the exercise until you are not afraid of shifting out anymore (it may take many shifts before getting used to it). Each time you shift out your subtle body will be in the prone position (that's how it is with me). Your perspective will be at the floor level. Be calm, get up, and move into the next room so that you won't be too close to your physical body and get drawn back in.

Those are the techniques I use. It may not seem like much but it is all you need. Getting out of body is not some elaborate mystery that you have to be a genius to solve. It's all fairly straightforward once you know the key components (the next chapter will break down these components in seven steps). As I've said before, it is mostly about conditioning, changing beliefs and getting over one's fears. If you are willing to put in the work, you are bound to get the desired outcome (and it may happen quicker than you anticipate).

After you have succeeded in being awake outside your flesh, it is best for the first few experiences to stay within your home as this place is familiar to you and will be of comfort. As you get more accustomed to the laws of inner reality and the finer body in which you find yourself, you can begin to extend your reach – venture outside, practice flying around your neighborhood, visit other cities and states, countries, or explore the universe if you can manage it. And, of course, you may move into even subtler realms for those enigmatic experiences that may well reach beyond description.

Summary: 7 Steps to a Conscious Projection

Here is my attempt at simplifying the process of consciously leaving the body. All of the steps are important so don't skip over any. If you truly want to go out of body and do so on a regular basis, this is as easy as it is probably going to get. Since you probably already have a strong desire to experience a projection, half the battle is already won. As this is a summary, I will be repeating myself to a large extent but it is necessary so that you can see what needs to be done in a condensed format.

1. Belief reconstruction. If you harbor negative beliefs that separating from your body is dangerous, against God's wishes, etc., or if you think the whole concept is silly and unlikely to be true, then you have some work ahead of you. You need an overhaul of your belief system. Your subconscious is keeping score and if you are waving around your fear flag – in whatever manner that may be – then you are making it clear that you are not mentally ready or prepared for this reality expansion experience. You're holding back; building a wall – you have issues that you will need to address first.

Functionally, you are equipped right now with everything you need to have an OBE and you do so nightly without remembering – you were designed with this ability, to return to your homebase as it were (being physical is really the peculiarity here, the anomaly). Since being physical is all you remember it may seem reckless and a bit dreadful to you that you would purposely separate from it, dive headlong into an "unknown" realm, but the choice is yours. If you are willing to practice each morning and work at what is holding you back, you will eventually be able to put your psyche in a suitable state in which a fully conscious projection will be attainable.

For most of us fear is the primary obstacle. It keeps us from venturing outside our skins because we slam on the brakes as soon as something outside our comfort zone begins to happen. Or we get a peek at the dark side of our psyche which scares us so thoroughly that we have second thoughts about the whole thing. Getting over this hump is not an easy feat. As I related earlier, I've had a few *I-want-my-mommy!* moments but these experiences occur rarely and will likely be rare for you as well if you are a fairly upbeat person. Holding the idea that something may attack you while out of body will probably keep you consciously flesh-locked. I've repeated the following statement many times but it is one of the most important things to remember – if you are in "trouble" you can easily go back to your body and awaken with just the thought to do so, or the heightened emotions you express will send you back instantaneously.

Keep in mind, the negative experiences you may encounter will be of your own making for the most part. That's the thing about being out of body, especially in the astral plane, it magnifies deep-seated fears, frustrations, etc., into whatever creative form is natural for the projector. What you are (your thoughts and subconscious thoughts, your beliefs) is what you will get. Negative or positive experiences are dependent upon you – you will manifest and attract what you concentrate upon. This same principle follows the physical plane as well (although in a much slower manner and in different ways) but unlike the physical plane you cannot be harmed; thus, there is nothing to fear in the non-physical realms, no matter what happens.

2. Keep a journal. I know, it's boring, and it's so much work. Get over it. Write down everything: your dreams, dream fragments, remote viewings, OBEs, the vibrational state and other pre-projection phenomena, spirit conversations, anything that pertains to the inner workings of YOU. The point is to uncover how you tick: the mechanisms, the nuts and bolts of your hidden life. Your job is to bring this other side of your existence into view and a journal will help you do that. As time goes on, you'll begin to remember more and more of what happens while you sleep, and you'll find that leaving the body gets that much easier. Maintaining a journal of your nonphysical activity serves as a super affirmation to your subconscious mind that you wish to continue experiencing and remembering such phenomena.

3. Read OBE literature. Before going to bed you should read a few passages from your favorite out-of-body book. The idea is to keep your mind freshly soaked with thoughts about separating from your body, floating above your bed, flying about, etc. This will help to induce a dream of this nature which may lead to a lucid dream and ultimately to a full-fledged out-of-body experience.

4. Affirmations (planting the seed). Before drifting off to sleep you should always state strongly to your subconscious mind your desire to experience an OBE. These should be spoken aloud or you can make an audio MP3 recording that repeats your affirmations. Use the suggestions I've given in the "Techniques" chapter or create your own personalized affirmations that resonate better with you.

5. Body relaxation. One of the most important things you must have in order to induce an OBE is a VERY RELAXED BODY. In other words, *your body must be asleep!* I wouldn't bother with trying to project without the body being in sleep mode first unless you are a master at meditation and body relaxation (some individuals claim they can project while jogging or just going for a walk but I think this must be extremely rare). I've never had any luck listening to relaxation CDs or audios that were designed specifically for out-of-body travel. This may work for others but it had practically no effect on me.

I found that the easiest way to obtain a relaxed body which is in the perfect condition for an out-of-body experience is by sleeping for six to eight hours. Then, all you will need to do is to allow your mind to awaken naturally without waking your body. As you first become aware or cognizant, as you first experience an inkling of the "white glimmer" (as I call it), do not open your eyes or move any part of your body. You will be able to do this with practice, don't worry! Once conditioned, the white glimmer will be used as a trigger for early morning OBEs. As you acknowledge the white glimmer occurring, it will serve as a signpost to you that your consciousness is awakening and projection is possible.

While you are in this hypnopompic state, it feels as though your body is comatose or encased in plaster. So, if you think about or try to move any part of your physical body whatsoever you will break that plaster condition and any chance for a conscious projection will be that much more remote. If you did move your body a tad, you can still recover that plaster state by not moving any more and allowing your body to fall back into sleep mode again. It will likely take many morning sessions before you get a handle on keeping the body still (asleep) while allowing your consciousness to brighten.

Finally, it is ideal to train yourself to be on your back (give yourself the suggestion before sleep that this will be the position you will be in as dawn breaks). For some reason almost all of my OBEs occur when I'm on my back – probably 90% of them. I'm not sure why but if I'm on my back it is more likely that the necessary conditions for leaving the body will be there. I think that being on my back somehow balances myself on that thin line of mind awake / body asleep mode.

6. Don't try too hard. It is important that you understand *not to try too hard* to leave the body. That may seem like a strange statement but you don't want to force an OBE – that will get you nowhere. Leaving the body is a delicate act. You need the proper mindset. For many, it is just when they give up on projecting after weeks or months of trying that they finally succeed. The reason for this is because they've dropped that hurried, trying-too-hard push and finally relax a bit while still keeping that strong desire in the background. You have to be open to projection, not fearful, and easy going. Know what you want, know that it will happen, and go with the flow.

Leaving the body is like playing a musical instrument. When you try too hard you become stiff and don't play well; when you slightly side-shift your thoughts and allow it to happen, the music flows easily and naturally through you. I also believe projecting is infinitely easier if you don't have a hectic life. I think you will find that the best projectors are carefree, silly, playful people (hippies / nature lovers / creative-artsy folk). A calm, peaceful mind, and a joy for life will go a long way towards your goal of regular (and happier) projections.

7. Separation. "The Morning Method" will give you the best shot at a conscious projection. After you have conditioned yourself to awaken without moving the body, you can begin to attempt separation from it. This is the true test: are you a wimp or a warrior? You can do this anyway you like, whatever feels right for you. I usually roll out of body. Some people like to float. But the actual process of separating confuses some people as they end up moving their physical body. If you are in the correct mode all it takes is the simple desire to float or to initiate the act of rolling off the bed and you will do so, unless you are blocking yourself or canceling your intentions out of fear. You make the move to roll out of body but then – almost at the exact moment –

you cancel it out, a sort of mind battle ensues. Fear has taken over – you are not separating from your body because a part of you keeps saying *NO*. You must get control of your thoughts – you cannot be half-hearted, you must be crystal clear in your objective.

Another approach that may be easier for the overly fearful, is this: When you first begin to awaken think of your consciousness moving in increments, clockwise or counterclockwise. You are not attempting to leave your body but learning to move your consciousness so that you can get a feel for it. Just imagine it revolving, a tiny increment at a time. You will learn that you can make a complete revolution. If sight is available you will actually see your perspective changing with each turn; without sight, you will still be able to feel yourself revolving. This consciousness-revolving technique may be easier for you as you are not dealing with separation and therefore you don't have the fears you may associate with separation. It is definitely an odd experience but not so jarring or overwhelming that you recoil in fright. Just continue to work with the manipulation of your consciousness, turning it slowly, one notch at a time. Once you have done this for a while you will be more comfortable with the idea of separating from your body.

Clearly, though, the most effective way to separate is to do it as soon as the "white glimmer" has been acknowledged. Immediately roll off the bed (or just stand up) and then get away from the physical body into the next room. You want to do this as quickly as possible. Don't lie in bed in the mind awake / body asleep state contemplating your situation. You need to program yourself that the "white glimmer" (the first light of wakefulness) means immediate action, to initiate a separation method and to get the heck out of there. The reason for this swiftness is twofold: because the hypnopompic state is of short duration (unless you have learned to prolong it), and to prevent an accidental reentry by being too close to the physical body (which is why you should move quickly into the next room or sufficiently away).

On the other hand, however, this is only a suggestion and may not be a good fit for you psychologically. It is for those who want a quick result and don't like to dawdle, and to have the best chance for a clean and sustained exit. You, however, may wish to separate at a more leis-urely pace. It is fine to hover in the mind awake / body asleep state as long as you need to (if you can manage it) and then ease yourself out-side your body when you are ready. You may have a few more fits and starts (shifting in and out of body), or maybe you won't. I don't always feel a tug on my physical body just because I am close to it. You won't know how it will go until you are out there.

For the first few OBEs you'll probably want to play around in your room for a bit, anyway – maybe take a gander at your physical body, practice some fancy acrobatics, or study the luminous form you cur-rently inhabit. Whatever you do, it is usually time well spent as everything out of body is always interesting in some way.

The above seven steps should get you out of body. It works for me. If you can't get out of body then you need to work on one or more of the seven steps above. Practice every morning, and remember to write down your progress. Soon you will be able to slip out of your skin, too, with your full consciousness, your everyday waking self, along for the ride.

Objective Reality
or Lucid Dreaming?

The most common question I get asked is: "What makes you
think you're not just dreaming?" My short answer is this: "I
just know," which certainly is not a very satisfying answer for the
doubting individual. It is not an easy task to explain to someone who
has never had a fully conscious OBE how one knows one is not "just
dreaming". Many people have had flying dreams and so they assume
that that is what I am referring to – except that I'm calling them out-of-

body experiences because, perhaps, I'm the gullible sort, or I have a screw loose. Although I do believe that most flying dreams (and dreams in general) take place apart from the physical body, it is necessary to differentiate these experiences from the *nondreaming* flying experiences. Even those who have had partial OBEs – projections where the mind is semi-awake – are often left with the feeling afterwards that it all was just too dreamlike to be more than that, and so they dismiss it (if they had taken the steps to acquire more consciousness the dream elements would have dispersed). Because of the unrealness of the experience, they begin to question the validity of OBEs altogether. It is only with a fully conscious projection where this all changes. The individual knows with every sense he has that he was not dreaming. He is stunned by the experience, by the stark realism, by the beauty, by the bright self-awareness seated firmly in his nonphysical head. He is elated because it was *REAL*, and no one could ever convince him otherwise.

The situation, however, becomes complicated when one attempts to prove to others that his experience is real by conducting experiments outside the body only to be smacked down when that proof proves evasive.

In my case, to find the definitive proof, I had conducted the following experiment. I had a stack of twenty-five 8" X 11" sheets of white typing paper wherein I had written a different number onto each sheet with a large black marker (numbers ranging from 1 to 25). Each night before bed I would close my eyes and shuffle the stack, place one random sheet on top (face up), and then place the stack under the bed at the foot of it. In the morning I would roll out of body, go to the end of the bed, get on my hands and knees and stick my etheric head underneath the bed so that I could read the number. Once I had seen the number I'd jump back into my body, wake up physically, then go to the end of the bed to verify. I did this experiment each morning for just over a week (one morning I had managed to do the experiment twice – I reshuffled the pages, got back into bed, into the hypnagogic state, and projected again). The final tally of this experiment: I didn't get any of the numbers correctly! You would think by chance alone I would've gotten at least one of them correctly, but no.

Disappointed, certainly. However, these results didn't sway me towards the belief that my OBEs were only dreams – not at all. I knew this wasn't the case. I had had my full consciousness during all of these target-number experiments, and I knew what lucid dreaming felt like and this wasn't it. What I needed to find out was what caused this miscommunication between realities.

The cause, of course, was me (my psyche). When conducting any kind of proof-seeking experiment in nonphysical reality you must be free of all conscious suggestions and expectations, as well as those pesky subconscious thoughts of which you are unaware. Unfortunately this is nearly impossible. This is why attempting to see target symbols while out of body, especially under controlled laboratory conditions, fail for the most part. The mere act of wanting to prove the reality of an OBE is pretty much setting yourself up.

This is the main reason why there are so few documented cases proving the reality of OBEs – it's not because it's all just a dream as those doubting individuals and sleep researchers have concluded, but because of the malleability of the nonphysical realm itself (which, actually, while in the the etheric plane, is merely a superimposing of one's thoughts over a stable physical reality; you are not actually changing the etheric environment, only overlaying it with one's thoughts). As this is a thought-responsive environment of an instantaneous nature, when you are seeking proof, you are creating a minefield (*mind*field) of conscious and subconscious expectation which leads to a false reading. Your thoughts are constantly and immediately being displayed over the nonphysical landscape, albeit rather subtly while in the etheric plane. In short, these accidental thoughts (coalescing furtively into form) are mucking with our proof-seeking endeavors.

The reality is, you will never see an exact copy of the physical world reflected in nonphysical reality. When you project from your body into your bedroom, for example, it will often appear that the room is the same as it is physically until you take a closer look and spot an anomaly or two. These anomalies can be quite clever and blend in so craftily they may go unnoticed. I had once gone out of body and saw a tall tin can sitting on my dresser that read *"Mc-Manon's"* in blue cursive lettering. This can did not belong here. I have never seen such a can in my life, but here it was, acting as though it had every right to be here.

These sly devils can appear anywhere. While projected over your local town, for example, it may appear the town is as you know it to be but upon closer inspection there may be some aspects of it that are out of whack – there may be a tree in front of a building where you know no tree should be, or a particular Victorian house that you have always known to be an ugly dark brown may now be a lovely traditional light green. These changes may be the subconscious handiwork of you, superimposing your thoughts and desires over the actual etheric landscape. In physical life, you may have wondered why the owners of that beautiful Victorian home would paint it such a drab color; but here, out of body, you have fixed that problem without realizing you have done so. Or, perhaps, you may be seeing an overlay of a different time frame when that Victorian home actually *was* a light green, or when there actually *was* a tree in front of that building.

You can see now how it can be tricky to find proof when the etheric landscape doesn't always conform perfectly to what is currently happening on the physical plane (as you subtly and sneakily superimpose it with your subconscious thoughts, or instigate a case of retrocognition). It is one thing to just stumble upon proof (much easier and reliable), but another thing altogether to go out *specifically* in search of proof. If one goes out searching for it you will likely be disappointed as your highly focalized expectations will create a false reflection of physical reality. You want to see physical reality as it really is and to not distort it with what you think it may be, in your attempt to *prove* something. If finding proof were an easy task there would be, by now, a gamut of verifiable documentation by scientific researchers and in general a stronger belief in the out-of-body experience by the common man.

Instead, we are left with the majority of society concluding that those who claim they can leave their bodies and freely roam the landscape of a higher dimension are a little more than a bit wonky. I don't blame them. How can you explain to someone who's never had a fully conscious projection the validity of the experience – that you know in your heart is *real* – if you cannot easily provide proof? And if you mention the peculiarities of the nonphysical landscape, how conscious and subconscious thought can overlay it, this leads them to further assert that the experience is, once again, "just a dream". Because, how can one be painting with thoughts and yet not be dreaming? How can one be fully conscious – even more awake than physically awake – and manifest thought into form, and yet be convinced he is not lucid dreaming? Why does he insist on believing that the nonphysical realm is independent of his mind, or exists in an objective reality, when he acknowledges that his subconscious mind is responsible for at least some of it?

So, then, what are the fundamental differences between OBEs and lucid dreaming? And is finding proof actually possible?

The most obvious difference between the two states is that of consciousness. With a lucid dream, although I do have all of my critical faculties intact, my self-awareness is still one step removed from normal consciousness (it is, as before stated, as though my dream body is a puppet that I am controlling from afar). With a fully conscious OBE, on the other hand, my self-awareness is firmly established at exactly where I stand (or float). I am using a first-person viewpoint – my wakefulness is exactly the same or better than my physical waking consciousness. I cannot stress this enough – in the same way that you do not need to ask yourself if you are lucid dreaming while physically awake, you do not need to ask yourself this when you are having a fully conscious out-of-body experience. You know that you are not dreaming. There is no wondering or doubting it; it is a fact as far as you are concerned.

Take my mother's first OBE as an example. You should know that my mother is the type of person (like myself, call it stubbornness) who will not go to a doctor unless there is a serious or life-threatening situation. She prefers to ride out any illness on her own without prescription drugs or the aid of a doctor, and let her body do the healing. But one night many years ago she awoke to find herself floating above her body near the ceiling. As a young woman she had never heard of astral projection or the out-of-body experience, and since she was certain she had not been dreaming she felt that something must be seriously wrong with her. A brain tumor, perhaps. She actually thought that that might be it. She made an appointment with a doctor and had a brain scan but there was nothing abnormal. She was perfectly healthy. It was only when my uncle gave her a copy of *Journeys Out of the Body* by Robert Monroe that everything suddenly made sense to her.

When was the last time you went to the doctor for a brain scan because you had an uncomfortable dream? Never, I'm sure. I think the last time my mother went to the doctor before this was to give birth. This experience was so incredibly out of the norm that she felt she *must* see a doctor as soon as possible.

In addition, when I dream – regularly or lucidly – the experience is usually of a bizarre, extremely action-packed, and insane nature: UFOs, odd creatures, dying in various ways, explosions, running for my life, numerous World War II scenarios, etc. Or the dreams are just plain nonsensical, as though I were trapped in a mental asylum and everything was distorted, cockeyed, and confusing. Contrast that with my etheric projections, which are almost exclusively of a quiet and peaceful temperament. It basically consists of me exploring, moving about as I wish, in a beautiful, serene, ethereal environment. Although I can get myself into strange situations (e.g., almost getting stuck in items, etc.), these experiences cannot be compared to the lunacy of dreaming. While etherically projected you simply won't encounter, say, a snarling Cerberus or a herd of Centaurs. The astral plane, however, is a different story. I think the reason the etheric plane is less suitable for this type of manifestation may have to do with its proximity to the physical plane, the denseness / lower vibration being incongruous to large-scale psychological stirrings (especially of the emotional, fear-based fantastical kind), unlike the astral plane, where its higher vibration / finer substance gives it a natural inclination towards wilder spontaneous creations and easy manipulation. If you happen upon angels, demons, fairies, elves, etc., you can bet you are in the astral plane (either in regular dream mode or conscious but hallucinating mode). These creatures will usually be spawned from your subconscious but they could be thought-forms created by others. Or you may be superimposing your assumptions or beliefs onto an individual (e.g., a guide / helper shown to you as an angel; this conversion may also be done by the guide himself for your benefit, as often seen in near-death experiences).

While lucid dreaming, you can control the characters in the dream, and you can control events, but you cannot do this during an etheric plane projection. The individuals you see moving about are independent of you and you cannot control what they do, what they say, where they go, etc. As you witness a physical event occurring before you (from your etheric vantage point) you are not able to alter that event in any way. It will unfold as it will, as you are only a spectator and not the creator. If these projections were actually lucid dreams, as many assert, than one would have control over every aspect of the experience, but clearly one does not in these particular experiences.

Another difference between an etheric projection and lucid dreaming is in the process of how each one occurs. With my morning method of projection I do not lose consciousness. I go from a waking state inside my physical body to the same waking state outside of it (and then take the steps for further awareness if needed). I simply get out of bed but leave my physical body behind. Contrarily, to arrive at a lucid dream, I am first in the sleep state with normal dreaming but then at some point become cognizant that I am dreaming.

Besides the unbroken line of consciousness with a self-induced projection, there are many other characteristics that differentiate it from a lucid dream. Chief among these are the vibrations that sometimes occur before a projection. Almost every frequent projector has experienced the vibration phenomenon at some point and most have numerous times (some every time they project). Are we all dreaming the same thing, a mass hallucination? Of course not. If you have never experienced the vibrational state at its most energetic it is simply not something anyone can adequately imagine beforehand. It doesn't matter how many out-of-body books you have read about it, or how many projectors you know personally who have described it to you, until you have experienced it yourself you do not have a full grasp of what it actually entails – how it really feels, and what a crazy, ridiculous ride it truly is. I don't think it's possible to mentally prepare yourself in advance for the intensity of it. When it happens for the first time you'll probably have such a massive psychological reaction to it that you will try to stop it immediately.

Another characteristic that projectors experience is the various sounds before and during exiting (often accompanying the vibrational state): whooshing, roaring, buzzing, etc. Are we all mass dreaming this, too? And the strange fog or mist that surrounds the physical body and the immediate vicinity? And the "stuck in mud" sensation as well? And the fact that you can look back and see your physical body in all its detail? And that you will instantly return to your body with the slightest twinge of fear or alarm? And the dual consciousness experience? And the 360 degree vision? Etc., etc.

Are all of these characteristics simply self-created by suggestion from the reading of OBE literature? No. Many individuals, like my mother, had never read any material at all about the phenomenon beforehand, or even heard about it. It was only afterwards that they sought out information to explain what had happened to them and were surprised to discover that they shared the same characteristics. Since these particular OBE accounts (of which a large body of them have been collected and documented in the last hundred years) could not have been dreamt up by suggestion, this alone demonstrates that the projection process is systematic, natural, and fundamental to all physical beings. These individuals, for whatever reason, just happened to be awake during the experience while the majority of us sleep through it.

A fully conscious out-of-body experience is as real as regular life – you are just as AWAKE. If you are unfamiliar with the phenomenon then you may think that you are actually using your physical body. That is, until you notice your physical body asleep on the bed! You wonder how this could be, how is this possible. This is all so unlike a dream that if you had never heard about the out-of-body experience you would have a terrible time processing it. Then a truly dreadful notion occurs to you: you wonder if perhaps you have died – *and suddenly you are back in the flesh.* You have no explanation for what had happened. You figure you might be crazy, or that something is deathly wrong with you. Therefore, off to the doctor you go!

Validating Your Projections

So, is proof possible? As mentioned before, the problem with obtaining proof is that once you begin the methodology for acquiring it – such as the use of target cards – you have, in your excitement and anticipation, built up an atmosphere of expectation which will likely result in a false outcome. However, fortunately, proof is still very much possible, you are just going about it the wrong way.

During your etheric plane projections, proof is all around you. There is no need for setting up target cards; instead, stumbling onto proof is how you are going to obtain your proof. By randomly discovering proof, you have not created any expectation beforehand and are seeing the environment mostly unmodified. Your psyche has not been given the chance to overlay the proof with a false envisage because you have already *seen* and *noted* the proof (the grubby paws of expectation was simply not in attendance to mess with your evidential data).

Thus, as you move about and enjoy your OBE, calmly take note of the particulars you happen upon, the small details you have never noticed in physical life. Don't project with the idea that you are going on a proof-hunt; that is setting yourself up again. Discovering proof should be secondary, happenstance. You are only nonchalantly observing while moving about your own home and to other areas (familiar and unfamiliar) in which you will have physical access later (so that you can compare regular reality against the minutiae you gathered nonphysically).

Right before my first OBE I had obtained some amount of proof with my remote viewing (proof enough to satisfy me, anyway), when I saw through that small hole in my mind's eye into the kitchen. There was my mother at the stove, who had made what appeared to me to be a cake but turned out to be meatloaf for my father (it looked just as I had seen it in the remote viewing, and its pan was of the same size and shape). I also saw the white box on the counter in the exact spot where I had seen it (which was a white box of donuts). This experience coincided at the same time in which my mother was actually in the kitchen cooking.

While projected, you have an endless supply of unobserved evidential data that you can gather which will confirm to you the objectivity of your experiences. It may not satisfy skeptics but if you were fully conscious during your projections then you probably already feel your OBEs were real and this is yet another validation. I would roll out of body with the notion to just have fun, and sometimes when I came across an object I would get right up to it and study the details (the details of which I had never noticed while physically oriented). There, on the floor, a pile of my clothes … I got down right next to it and calmly studied and memorized the curvatures, the twists and shapes, how one specific item laid upon another in a particular manner, etc. When I was satisfied that I held a good representation of the pile of clothes in my mind (a mental snapshot), I would jump back into my body, awaken physically, and get up to verify. The pile of clothes on my floor was exactly the same.

Another time I left my body early in the morning and studied myself sleeping on the bed. My head was straight back against the pillow, almost vertical like it would be if I were sitting up (it looked very uncomfortable), and I had both hands clutching the blanket which was pressed against my chin just under my bottom lip. I lay back in coincidence with my body and made absolutely sure that I kept still while I awakened physically. I opened my eyes and observed my body's position. Everything was precisely the same as I had seen it from my projected vantage point – the way my head was propped up, the position of my body in relation to the bed, the blanket up to my chin under my lip. There wasn't a single thing that wasn't as I had seen it. It was an exact copy.

Again, understandably, this is not something that will convince a disbeliever; it was done for my own curiosity. I realize an argument can be made that I'd held a subconscious memory of my body's position. Nonetheless, this is something you should try at least once as it is quite interesting and eerie to be outside your body, to see it sleeping in a particular arrangement and then to verify that it was indeed sleeping in that exact manner.

More interesting is to happen upon evidential data from a great distance from where you are physically that can be verified by another person. In this example, I projected a distance of about eighty miles to my parents' home. My brother was living there at the time and I went into his bedroom and noticed a scrap of paper laying atop his dresser. Without touching it (very key), I saw two things written on it: a girl's first name and beneath that was a phone number. Unfortunately I did not attempt to memorize the number (which, of course, would have made this example a much better proof) but I did have the girl's name. When I phoned him the next day my brother was thoroughly astonished (and probably a bit creeped out). He confirmed that there was a scrap of paper atop his dresser onto which a girl's first name was written and that there was a phone number written beneath that. Although he said I had gotten the name correctly it was actually abbreviated or contracted on the paper (e.g., from Catherine to Cathy). You could say that I saw more true information than what was written on the paper, as I saw her full given first name, even though on the paper it was written in its contracted form. I don't know why I saw it as a whole rather than the contraction. I do consider this a win – or at least a partial win – because I did, in fact, get her actual name correctly, even though I had read it slightly differently on the paper (not contracted), and the paper was located where I had seen it (atop the dresser). I did not know of this girl's existence prior to this OBE.

In the above example, I stated that it was "very key" to have not touched the scrap of paper. I believe one of the reasons why my target card experiments failed so completely was because, on several occasions, I had picked up the 8" X 11" sheet of paper (its etheric counterpart) in my attempt to read it. The reason for having done so was because my bedroom would often be so enshrouded with that ectoplasmic fog that I couldn't make out the target number on the paper. It didn't occur to me that, by lifting the paper, I might be disturbing what was actually written on it – until, on one occasion, the target number began sliding around on the paper like an egg in a frying pan. However, even in those instances where I hadn't touched the paper I still did not get the target number correctly. Although my room was frequently foggy, I would not leave until I was certain that I had the correct number (but, as it turned out, I was still wrong every time).

If you want to try the target card experiment yourself, your chances of success would probably increase if you place the target card in another room away from your physical body (to avoid the ectoplasmic fog problem), and if you remember to never touch the target card when attempting to read it. In addition, you should never leave the remaining cards underneath the pile as I had. There could possibly be a telepathic bleed-through, or one's perception may be able to pass beyond the first card to see another, thus rendering the experiment void. Even with all of these precautions you will still have the issue of expectation mucking with your proof, which would be your main adversary.

Once again, I believe you would be better off to just let the proof present itself to you. A good procedure is to visit someone during an OBE that you haven't seen for a while, to a house that you have never been to – this would offer you plenty of chances to observe things and situations you did not know about beforehand and that you can verify later by phoning them.

My mother once projected from Oregon to Arizona to check in on my oldest sister who had moved there (perhaps intuitively sensing that her daughter needed her), and what she saw startled and worried her. My sister, who has never been overweight as far as I can remember, was now rather *huge*, at least according to what my mother saw during this OBE. There was my sister, standing in the foyer of her house beneath a black chandelier, and she was clearly overweight, shockingly so. My mother immediately phoned her and found out that my sister had indeed gained a lot of weight because she was pregnant – a fact that none of us knew about – and the due date wasn't far off. A few weeks later my mother took a plane to Arizona to be with her for the birth (this was my sister's first child) and when she arrived she noticed that same black chandelier hanging in the foyer (other than from her OBE, she had never seen or knew about the chandelier as this was her first physical trip to Arizona). This is a good example of simple observation (viewing my sister's overweight appearance and the surroundings) without the mindset of expectancy distorting the experience.

After you have validated a few experiences, obtaining further proof will likely not be a priority for you. As you become a more frequent projector and have been around the block, so to speak, the basic experience of being outside your body with full consciousness is validation enough. By now you have concluded that you are indeed functioning outside of dreams, in a realm independent of yourself, and that you have other interests above gathering proof during your precious OB time. Nevertheless, you should always be a good observer and make sure to write down everything in exacting detail into your journal. Although pursuing OBE validation may no longer be necessary to you, documenting these details can help with recall and to see the connections you may have not noticed between experiences.

In summation, if you still find it difficult to distinguish between an OBE and a lucid dream, ask yourself how aware were you *really*. Were you cognizant of the fact that you had a physical life and that your body was currently asleep? Could you recall anything about this physical life? Your name, your parents names, what you do for a living? Would you say you were just as aware and awake as you are in regular waking life? If the answers to these questions are "no," then you were lucid dreaming (still a valid projection but you were surrounded in thought constructions). While lucid dreaming, although you have a heightened awareness and know that you are awake, consciousness is simply not the same. Once full consciousness is experienced it will be obvious to you how far removed from a dream it is.

The Astral Jukebox

From nearly the very beginning, after only having had a few conscious projections, I discovered something that is apparently unique – or at least not as widely known – which I later began to refer to as "The Astral Jukebox". Surprisingly, in all of the OBE books I've read I have never come across any mention of this. For something so prominent in my OBEs, so blatant and constant, it is strange that I appear to be the only one experiencing it (although I'm sure that's not the case). The Astral Jukebox is with me now on nearly every excursion, whether its an etheric projection or an astral projection (and during remote viewings as well if I desire it). Basically, what this is is the ability to play *any* song that you have ever heard by simply thinking of it. And when I say play, I mean the actual complete song as recorded by the artist. The exact song, no different than what is on the CD or in your iTunes. Hundreds if not thousands of songs available, any of which can be accurately played whenever you want, as loudly or as softly as you want, for your listening enjoyment as you meander through the OB environment. Don't confuse this with that faded song you may have puttering in your head during physical waking consciousness. Again, The Astral Jukebox experience is no different than turning on your stereo and listening to a specific CD; you will hear it exactly the same way while out of body. Actually, the quality is much better, crisper and clearer, as we are not dealing with a clumsy physical device – a stereo – in which to play the music. It is as though the music is blasted down from the cosmos or some heavenly realm into your own personal space as you move about in your explorations (at least, I hope no one else can hear it; I usually play it quite loud and I wouldn't want to annoy the entire nonphysical population with my musical tastes).

To turn it on is simple. Once out of body (or even *in* body, as long as you are in the mind awake / body asleep state), all that you do is think of a song. You barely have to think much about it really, just a little to get it started, and then it will run its course without any more effort. You can adjust the "volume control" by thinking that you want it *louder louder louder* (the volume increases with each "louder" that you command) or for lower volume, use *lower lower lower* or *softer softer softer*; it doesn't matter which words you use as it is the intent that makes it change. The sound quality is truly amazing and it is ridiculous how loud you can turn it up (no amplifier on earth can beat it) and there is no fear of rupturing your ear drums as you are not physically hearing anything.

Furthermore, besides your own collection of songs that you have heard and copied to your subconscious mind, I've discovered that you can listen to complete songs which aren't physically available. These are songs by famous artists that have never been recorded on Earth and yet, somehow, miraculously, they are here for your nonphysical listening pleasure. For example, I discovered a song called "Ode to Peace" by Janis Joplin. You would think by the title it would be a mellow tune but it was actually a very hard rock, aggressive song. Joplin demanding peace *NOW!* kind of thing. It was fantastic (her voice was top-notch). A complete song in every way that doesn't exist on Earth (as far as I can tell), but here it was, accessible to me from The Astral Jukebox.

These "nonexistent" songs will begin playing on their own accord, as though my subconscious, knowing my favorite bands or the type of music I enjoy, is offering up suggestions to me. Other songs of this type include a beautiful and somewhat eerie Tool song which was quite long in duration; Thom Yorke of Radiohead singing about a "wandering cloud"; an acoustic version of "Back in Black" by AC/DC (this one may be available on Earth somewhere but I couldn't find it); a Cowboy Junkies ballad, etc.

Sometimes I accidentally play a song completely outside my musical tastes (I guess a particular memory or incident will trigger any old song to be played). Or a song from my childhood that I used to love will pop up out of nowhere (e.g., "Fire and Rain" by James Taylor, some Creedence Clearwater Revival, etc.).

I can understand how my subconscious stores every song that I've ever heard (although that's miraculous in itself), but from where did these unknown songs come? Since these are fully realized songs with complete and sensible lyrics, using the actual voices and musical talents of these bands, perhaps all of these songs (physically recorded or not) are actually coming from the so-called Akashic Records and my subconscious has nothing to do with it (aside from picking through it and offering suggestions). The Akashic Records is purported to be a nonphysical "place" in which all knowledge is preserved and accessible. This energetic library is what Edgar Cayce apparently accessed through trance to locate specific information to treat his patients. As I

have had many – seemingly accidental – experiences with nonphysical books while remote viewing, books on a wide variety of topics and
genres (e.g., metaphysics, novels, poetry, etc.), I must have been
tuning into this musical archive in a similar manner. As there is no
conscious decision on my part to retrieve these specific songs since I
hadn't known they even existed, it must be done by another portion of
my consciousness of which I am completely unaware. These unknown
songs are all from musicians I already enjoy so my discovery of them
is unlikely to be random or by chance. Whether I am somehow the creator of these songs or they are actually from the Akashic Records, I do
not know.

Maybe Janis Joplin did create a song called "Ode to Peace" at one
point in her life but never recorded it (performed it only at some con-
cert or in a private session) but the psychic imprint is now available in
these records. Or maybe, after death, she wrote and performed this
song in the astral realm and it exists now forever nonphysically (creation / using one's talents doesn't stop just because you are no longer
physically focused). Seth says that all novels ever written exist now in
their own dimensions, that every idea continues to exist, and this
would go for songs as well.

Some items I access do seem random in that I don't see a connection to me, such as a hardcover book about the atrocities in China that
just suddenly appeared before me during a remote viewing. Many
books I see I have no interest in and I don't know why I stumble upon
them. I suppose it is not unlike one browsing in a physical library and
picking random books off a shelf, except I'm not purposely – consciously – choosing many of these items. They are thrust upon me, for
perhaps some unknown reason.

The Askashic Records idea does make the most sense for this phenomena (of retrieving new information). I find it hard to believe that I,
alone, am responsible for the creation of "Ode to Peace" and all of the
other heretofore unknown songs that I've listened to (considering how
complex some of these songs are, all of the instruments involved, the
lyrics, etc). How could I create all of these songs on the fly, with no

conscious effort? These are some of the most amazing songs I've ever heard and for me to take credit for them seems ridiculous. But maybe I am simply underestimating the skills I possess within the hidden portions of my psyche.

Interestingly, The Astral Jukebox is much more than just a player. I discovered that I can strip out the vocals from any song so that I can sing along with the music while I'm enjoying my OBE. I call this "Astral Karaoke". For example, for the song "Very Ape" by Nirvana I removed Kurt's voice completely and put my voice in its place while the song played. I was in full control of how I wanted to sing it, with as much power as I wanted, but the voice was still characteristically mine (not Kurt's), and it was of a much higher quality than I could ever manage in physical life. This shows me that at least the manipulation of a song is very easy while in an altered state. I did the same to other songs, such as AC/DC's "Hells Bells" (ripping out Brian Johnson's voice and replacing it with my own). When you remove a voice there is absolutely no trace of it left in the song afterwards (it is done instantly, just with the simple desire for the voice to be removed, leaving the rest of the song intact).

Because it is so easy to manipulate a song in this manner, it makes me wonder if I *am* actually creating these unknown songs. Perhaps it is true that a much more talented part of me is doing this on a level of which I am unaware, lurking just out of view of my conscious thoughts. Perhaps this is the same portion of consciousness that autistic savants utilize, who have this great capacity for art or music without any formal training; they are somehow able to focus within this state easily and tap into their innate potentials as effortlessly as one breathes. The main trait of nearly all savants is an extraordinary memory, such as being able to play any song on the piano after only having heard the song once. This is not unlike the capability I have while in the mind awake / body asleep state, as far as being able to retrieve any song I've ever heard and replay it exactly as it was recorded by the artist. If only I could have this prodigious memory while physically awake!

Astral Karaoke is not only great fun but serves another purpose – to keep my mind preoccupied while exploring during an OBE. I find that singing extends the out-of-body experience by keeping me calm. It makes me happy and at peace to have any music I want beaming down upon me, a soundtrack to accompany the beautiful ethereal landscape that surrounds me. If not using Astral Karaoke, I will just sing along with any song unaltered which is what I do most often. Listening to music is such a large part of my physical life that it's no wonder it carries over into my OBEs. I'm nearly always humming some tune, and I can't drive without music playing, so my love for music is what made it such an easy and obvious discovery for me while outside my body.

I have little doubt that any one can play music during an OBE if the desire is there. Once you realize it's possible it should be no problem for you as long as you are in the mind awake / body asleep state. No other skill is needed as far as I know. Just think of a favorite song and that's it – your own personal Astral Jukebox will begin to play.

Conclusion

The most profound reason to induce an out-of-body experience is for the knowledge that death is an illusion, that our physical body is not what makes us alive. I hope this book has shown to you at least a little of your true immortality status, and that those loved ones you may have lost to death live on as strongly and as brightly as they ever did physically. As I stated in the Introduction, having the ability to consciously leave your body is your right. Each of us is equipped with this ability *now*, with the inner senses to see the invisible. Learning to shift your awareness will expand your concept of reality and allow you to utilize a larger portion of you. All that is needed is the in-clination – the knowing that it is possible and to put forth the effort.

This book is especially for those who believe that life is chaotic and random and basically meaningless, that one life is lived and then you are gone forever. This is no way to live. What would be the point of such a brief existence? – to be given intelligence and feelings and cre-ativity only for it to be taken away? It makes no sense. The real you does not consist of atoms and molecules. Your consciousness does not include a capacity for extinction. You will continue on, whether you want to or not.

When your physical death does occur, it will be, of course, a diffi-cult experience no matter the circumstance, but by learning to project your consciousness now you will be acclimating to the same condi-tions you will meet after death. By knowing the basics of conscious-ness survival before your physical demise and by having actually prac-ticed the various modes of locomotion in the nonphysical environment, you will be far more composed and accepting of your condition than the majority of the human populous. Obviously, since you are reading this book and have at least an interest in the out-of-body experience, you are already ahead of the game, so to speak.

Even if you never manage to project consciously while physically alive you do have a fair idea of what an OBE is like and this will be of assistance to you in the afterlife. Likewise, recognizing now that a bib-lical heaven and hell does not exist apart from an individual's psycho-logical condition will enable you to bypass such thought constructions in death. You will be able to witness the true afterlife environment and understand your situation clearly so that you may get on with things. No need for mind games when you have other pressing matters, like having your questions answered by guides / teachers and locating your loved ones.

For those desiring a heaven, there are heights for us to reach / ex-pansions of consciousness that we can't even conceive of yet but there is no end point, no finish line to cross. As Seth says, we are all in a state of becoming and always will be. Heaven is in the experiences and self-discoveries and the company you keep. When death comes, you need not fear it as nothing is ever lost.

In the meantime, enjoy the life you have now, be mindful of your thoughts, know that you have the power to change even the most deep-rooted beliefs, and that, with a little practice and on a fairly frequent basis, you may step fully conscious across the threshold and into the "unknown".

OBE Survey

Several years ago I placed a survey on my web site which asked 21 basic questions to those who have experienced out-of-body travel. A total of 1,136 people responded. Here are the results:

Q1. How many OBEs have you had?	Respondents	Percentage
One.	214	19.00%
Two.	146	13.00%
Three.	120	11.00%
Four.	55	5.00%
5 or more.	217	19.00%
10 or more.	169	15.00%
50 or more	80	7.00%
100 or more.	46	4.00%
500 or more.	24	2.00%
1000 or more.	19	2.00%
No answer.	46	4.00%

Q2. How much awareness do you usually have during an OBE?	Respondents	Percentage
Fully or mostly aware.	707	62.00%

Semi-aware.	316	28.00%
Barely aware.	82	7.00%
No answer.	31	3.00%

Q3. Are your OBEs usually spontaneous or willed?	Respondents	Percentage
Spontaneous.	707	62.00%
Willed.	357	31.00%
No answer.	72	6.00%

Q4. What position is your physical body usually in when you project?	Respondents	Percentage
On back.	710	62.00%
On side.	196	17.00%
On stomach.	87	8.00%
Sitting up.	80	7.00%
No answer.	63	6.00%

Q5. Prior to a projection, which, if any, of these sounds have you heard?	Respondents	Percentage
Buzzing / Humming.	897	79.00%
Roaring.	255	22.00%
Voices.	368	32.00%
Whistling.	92	8.00%
Music.	146	13.00%
Singing.	62	5.00%

Bells ringing.	97	9.00%
None.	338	30.00%

Q6. Have you experienced The Vibrational State?	Respondents	Percentage
Yes.	681	60.00%
No.	410	36.00%
Not sure.	45	4.00%

Q7. Have you seen through your closed eyelids prior to an OBE?	Respondents	Percentage
Yes.	621	55.00%
No.	448	39.00%
Not sure.	67	6.00%

Q8. Have you experienced Catalepsy / Sleep Paralysis?	Respondents	Percentage
Yes.	815	72.00%
No.	286	25.00%
Not sure.	35	3.00%

Q9. Have you experienced Remote Viewing?	Respondents	Percentage
Yes.	480	42.00%
No.	546	48.00%
Not sure.	110	10.00%

Q10. Have you experienced Lucid Dreaming?	Respondents	Percentage
Yes.	903	79.00%
No.	151	13.00%
Not sure.	82	7.00%

Q11. Which separation method do you most commonly use?	Respondents	Percentage
Fly out or Lift out.	531	47.00%
Roll out.	135	12.00%
Slide out.	58	5.00%
Sink.	55	5.00%
Not sure or other.	357	31.00%

Q12. Have you seen your physical body during an OBE?	Respondents	Percentage
Yes.	443	39.00%
No.	616	54.00%
Not sure.	77	7.00%

Q13. What degree of control do you have during your OBEs?	Respondents	Percentage
Very good.	143	13.00%
Good.	406	36.00%
Poor.	330	29.00%
Very poor.	180	16.00%

No answer.	77	7.00%

Q14. Have you experienced any of the following during an OBE?	Respondents	Percentage
Foggy vision.	484	43.00%
Sluggish movement / heaviness.	461	41.00%
360 degree vision.	240	21.00%
Strong winds or astral currents.	201	18.00%
Stuck in objects (ceiling, walls, etc.)	172	15.00%
None.	244	21.00%

Q15. What does your subtle body usually appear to be wearing?	Respondents	Percentage
What I wore to bed.	162	14.00%
Everyday clothes (that I own).	120	11.00%
Everyday clothes (that I don't own).	73	6.00%
Something strange.	13	1.00%
Nothing, I'm nude.	83	7.00%
I don't know.	685	60.00%

Q16. Have you had an encounter with a spirit or being during an OBE?	Respondents	Percentage
Yes, a friendly encounter.	197	17.00%
Yes, an unfriendly encounter.	124	11.00%
Both friendly & unfriendly encounters.	239	21.00%
No.	576	51.00%

Q17. Which senses have you used during an OBE?	Respondents	Percentage
Sight.	1040	92.00%
Sound.	766	67.00%
Touch.	612	54.00%
Smell.	211	19.00%
Taste.	140	12.00%
None.	28	2.00%

Q18. Have you been able to prove that an OBE wasn't a dream?	Respondents	Percentage
Yes.	445	39.00%
No.	207	18.00%
Never tried.	405	36.00%
No answer.	79	7.00%

Q19. How would you characterize most of your OBEs?	Respondents	Percentage
Pleasant.	884	78.00%
Unpleasant.	168	15.00%
No answer.	84	7.00%

Q20. Would you like to continue to have OBEs?	Respondents	Percentage
Yes.	1051	93.00%
No.	37	3.00%

No answer.	48	4.00%

Q21. Do you believe consciousness survives death?	Respondents	Percentage
Yes.	868	76.00%
No.	24	2.00%
Maybe.	207	18.00%
No answer.	37	3.00%

References

Journeys Out of the Body by Robert A. Monroe

Astral Projection: A Record of Out-of-Body Experiences by Oliver Fox

The Projection of the Astral Body by Sylvan Muldoon

Seth, Dreams, and Projections of Consciousness by Jane Roberts

Seth Speaks by Jane Roberts

Journal of the American Society of Psychical Research, (article) by Prescott F. Hall

The Gateway Experience by The Monroe Institute

The Other Side of Death by Charles Leadbeater

"Treatise on Astral Projection" (online article) by Robert Bruce

Recommended Reading

Journeys Out of the Body by Robert A. Monroe

Far Journeys by Robert A Monroe

Ultimate Journey by Robert A. Monroe

The Projection of the Astral Body by Sylvan Muldoon

Astral Projection: A Record of Out-of-Body Experiences by Oliver Fox

Seth, Dreams, and Projections of Consciousness by Jane Roberts

The Seth Material by Jane Roberts

Seth Speaks by Jane Roberts

The Nature of Personal Reality: A Seth Book by Jane Roberts

The following books I haven't yet read but are well liked by others and may be of interest to you:

Adventures Beyond the Body by William Buhlman

The Secret of the Soul by William Buhlman

Projections of the Consciousness by Waldo Vieira

Leaving the Body by D. Scott Rogo

Quotes Used In This Book

"... you are "dead" now - and as dead as you will ever be." – From the book *Seth Speaks: The Eternal Validity of the Soul*. Copyright 1972 by Jane Roberts. Reprinted with permission of New World Library, Novato, CA. www.newworldlibrary.com

"Our ordinary consciousness shows us only one specific view of reality. When we learn to close off our senses momentarily and change the focus of awareness, other quite valid glimpses of an interior universe begin to show themselves." – From the book *Seth, Dreams and Projections of Consciousness* by Jane Roberts. Reprinted with permission of New Awareness Network Inc, Manhasset, NY. www.sethcenter.com

"Death is not real, even in the Relative sense – it is but Birth to a new life – and You shall go on, and on, and on, to higher and still higher planes of life, for aeons upon aeons of time." – the Three Initiates, The Kybalion

"A vegetable diet tends to loosen the vibric matter of the astral body ..." – Prescott F. Hall, *Journal of the American Society of Psychical Research*

Exploring Your Inner Reality

About the Author

Jonas lives in the Pacific Northwest. For more information, you may visit his web site at: www.JonasRidgeway.com. If you have some time, please consider leaving a review at Amazon.com. Thank you!

Made in the USA
San Bernardino, CA
24 February 2018